环球卓越
www.geedu.com

谭松
李

MW01706703

4周攻克雅思口语周计划

英语周计划系列丛书
ENGLISH WEEKLY PLAN SERIES

机械工业出版社
CHINA MACHINE PRESS

“英语周计划系列丛书”是针对我国读者的英语学习特点开发的、以“周”为谋篇布局单位、以“日”为具体实施单元的极具特色的英语辅导用书，具有思维创新、规划科学、目标明确、讲练结合、直击实战等特点。《4周攻克雅思口语周计划》是本系列针对IELTS的一个分册。

编者从雅思口语部分的题型特点和设题规律出发，针对考生复习中经常遇到的问题，为考生提供了一个完整的IELTS口语4周复习方案，每周安排7天（星期一至星期日），合计28天。第一周是7天入门，为您全面解析雅思口语；第二周是7天基础，为您精讲7套口语真题；第三周是7天强化，细致讲解7大雅思口语考试重点；第四周是7天冲刺，设置了7套模拟试题，检验学习成果。4周的安排，目标明确，科学合理，帮助考生理清复习思路，最终成功通过考试。

图书在版编目（CIP）数据

4周攻克雅思口语周计划/谭松柏主编．—北京：机械工业出版社，2011.8

（英语周计划系列丛书/谭松柏丛书主编）

ISBN 978-7-111-35585-4

Ⅰ．①4… Ⅱ．①谭… Ⅲ．①IELTS—口语—自学参考资料 Ⅳ．①H319.9

中国版本图书馆CIP数据核字（2011）第159495号

机械工业出版社（北京市百万庄大街22号 邮政编码100037）

责任编辑：孙铁军

封面设计：墨格文慧

责任印制：杨 曦

北京双青印刷厂印刷

2011年8月第1版第1次印刷

184mm×260mm·13.5印张·350千字

0 001－6 000册

标准书号：ISBN 978-7-111-35585-4

ISBN 978-7-89433-077-2（光盘）

定价：39.80元（1CD）

凡购本书，如有缺页、倒页、脱页，由本社发行部调换

电话服务

社服务中心：（010）88361066

销 售 一 部：（010）68326294

销 售 二 部：（010）88379649

读者购书热线：（010）88379203

网络服务

门户网：http://www.cmpbook.com

教材网：http://www.cmpedu.com

丛 书 序

现如今的中国人，上学不再满足于清华、北大，工作也不仅放眼于国企。而是走向一个更为宽广的世界——出国深造和就业。这是中国政治、经济、文化发展的结果，是好事，利国利民，利己利人。然而并非每个有出国梦想的人都能如愿以偿，很多人都被雅思这个拦路虎拦在了国门以内。

由于雅思考核学生听说读写的综合运用能力，这与中国传统的英语教学完全不接轨。尽管近年来中国的外语教学有了很大的改进和发展，但苦于没有语言环境，教学和学习效果依然不理想。加之教育改革周期长，效果缓慢，很多中国考生题做了不少，词汇记了无数，语法也学了很多，但一旦落实到应用，尤其是听说和写作，就最多只能是中式英语，这不符合雅思的考核标准。因此，很多中国考生都万事俱备，只欠雅思，但这雅思一分难求，所以很多考生只能望洋兴叹。虽心有不甘，但也只能脚踏实地走进英语课堂，走遍各个培训学校，听遍所有名师课堂。虽感觉老师们说的很有道理，感觉找到了救命稻草，但是，回到家中，冷静下来，却发现自己依然不会说英语，也听不懂，单词记不住，好不容易记住的那些，可能又忘了。

殊不知，语言学习是技能学习，和学开车、学游泳是一个道理。那就是，要想学好外语，必须增加练习，光听“教练”讲道理是不够的。考生在听完名师讲解雅思考试规律和复习技巧以后，还要坐下来，安静地看看书，从中获取养分，夯实英语基本功才是硬道理。不能抱着侥幸心理，想着混过雅思。而应借雅思这个东风，真正把英语水平提高，毕竟，走出国门后，就得靠英语生存、学习和工作了，那时多少分不再是硬道理。

英语的学习必须是听说读写词汇并进，很多考生屡考不过是因为缺乏严密的计划。而且，三天打鱼两天晒网，语言的学习在没有形成能力之前，往往一日不练十日空。因此，要想学好外语，还要作好科学的规划，并按这个规划去执行。很多考生要么完全不知道怎么学习，要么是盲从别人的方法，或是众说纷纭，不知所从。

“英语周计划系列丛书”是在分析考生的现状和种种困难的基础上形成的一整套完善的雅思复习计划。本系列丛书以提高考生英语应试水平、迅速提高雅思分数为目的，一举两得。雅思周计划共 5 本书，囊括了听说读写四大雅思考试板块，并涵盖学习英语的基本功：词汇。这 5 本书依次是：**《4 周攻克雅思听力周计划》**、**《4 周攻克雅思口语周计划》**、**《4 周攻克雅思阅读周计划》**、**《4 周攻克雅思写作周计划》**、**《4 周攻克雅思词汇周计划》**。

之所以叫周计划，是因为每本书都是以周为单位进行学习。其实，攻克雅思并非有多难，难就难在没有掌握技巧和方法，而本套丛书通过 4 周完整缜密的规划，将听、说、读、写并进，再辅以词汇，引领考生攻克雅思考试大关！

本系列丛书特点如下：

- **系统全面，涵盖雅思考试听说读写四大板块**。让雅思考试备考一气呵成，自成体系。
- **计划科学、完整、缜密，可操作性强**。每本书按 4 周进行，每周 7 天，每天任务具体、清晰、充实。考生无须再去苦恼该干什么，不该干什么。

- **科学的应试备考过程，从易到难，循序渐进**。每本书的第一周是“引进门”，让考生对雅思考试技能迅速了解；第二周是“打基础”，让考生基本功得到迅速夯实；第三周则是“技巧强化”，迅速提升考生语言水平，为考试作好充足的准备；而第四周则是“模拟考场”，让考生每天如战马驰骋，实战沙场，以达到考前最佳状态。
- **一书在手，众生皆宜**。这是本丛书的又一大特色。无论是从未涉足雅思考试的新手，还是久经沙场的“考鸭”，本丛书均能满足其需求，尤其是对于那些急于攻克雅思考试并渴求获取雅思高分的考生，本丛书更是书海中的首选！

每每在讲课之余，我都能碰到心急如焚的考生；每当看到他们那种求助的眼神，我都暗下决心要为他们做点什么。我也曾是一名外语学习者，也有过和他们一样的困惑和迷茫，但如今，我已是一名从事外语教学多年的老师，责任感和使命感促使我必须拿出切实的行动。在全国著名的培训机构——**环球卓越**的大力组织下，一批和我一样热心于雅思教学的师资团队走到了一起，用我们多年的教学成果，共同铸就了我们这套丛书——雅思周计划系列！

路，总是在延伸，一望无尽；但是，路，既有畅通无阻，也有曲折迂回。真心希望，这套周计划能让众多雅思考生少一点犹豫，少一点徘徊，少一点弯路，尽量把大好的青春年华用在有用的事情上。更希望众多的雅思考生，能够成为一名有志的中国学子，早日走出去，在实现自己梦想的同时，也为祖国富强添砖加瓦。我这区区外语教师，也算是不枉十年寒窗了。

谭松柏

2011年元旦于北京

前　　言

一对一的、纯英语母语的雅思口语面试，你准备好了吗？

本书通过4周的安排，将你从门外引入门内，由入门到熟悉，从强化到冲刺，最后一举攻克雅思口语考试！

第一周：7天入门，全面解析雅思口语考试。很多考生并不了解何谓雅思口语考试，甚至连考试流程都不清楚，从一开始就将自己和高分绝缘。针对众多考生薄弱之处，本周详细讲解了雅思口语考试流程，包括考试内容、考题特点、评分标准、如何备考及如何获取高分。所谓知己知彼，方能百战不殆。

第二周：7天基础，做透7套雅思口语真题。真题是检验和校正自己应试的最基本的能力。每天一套真题，同时将真题及自我评分表、模板答案、深度剖析真题话题以及拓展话题安置到每天的复习中，让考生深入透彻地了解雅思口语考试中第一部分的常考话题，全面掌握常考话题必备的语言基础。

第三周：7天强化，熟悉7大雅思口语考试重点。本周是雅思口语学习的强化阶段，分别以雅思口语考试的重点话题，即：人物描写、地点描写、物体描写、事件描写、故事描写、活动描写、经历描写为主线，一天一个重点，全面掌握雅思口语考试第二部分问题的回答思路，积累最为常见的答题模板和语言素材。

第四周：7天冲刺，掌握雅思口语考试7大难点。本周所讲的7大难点是雅思考试的7个常考话题，也是第三部分的7大考点，这7个话题分别是：animal，place，law，building，course，change，job。这7个话题在口语一、二、三部分都经常考到，因此它们是重点，但由于话题的问题往往刁钻古怪，让考生不知如何作答，从而影响考试的整体印象分。为了解决这个问题，本周一天一个话题，逐一攻克，力图让考生在深度学习这些话题的同时能够举一反三，直至全面攻克！

本书循序渐进，真正做到“周周有进步，日日有提升”，是一本市面上难得的雅思考前辅导书。

参加本书编写的还有詹圣麒、詹景祺、石茜、郭肇焱、刘敏、李兰荣、尹航、修苗苗、张玲、陈阳、潘秀英、刘晓蓉、李德标、何光锋、梁莉娟、孟宪华、许少雄、David Speary。

希望本书能成为您备考路上的好帮手！

编者

2011年5月于北京

目　　录

4周攻克

雅思口语周计划

第一周　7天入门：全面解析雅思口语

雅思考试非常注重考生语言实际运用能力，其口语采取一对一的面试形式，而且考官的母语全都是英语。很多中国考生考试成绩不理想，究其原因，主要是对雅思口语考试了解不够，有的甚至连考试流程都了解不够，更不用说该如何应对每个部分的考题。

在复习备考雅思口语的第一周，要从各个方面全面了解雅思口语，做到胸有成竹，才能马到成功。首先要了解的是雅思口语包括哪些部分，每个部分考题有哪些特点，该如何准备每一部分，考官以什么样的标准来打分，以及该如何拿到高分。以上这些，在备考之初，都必须全面了解。

星期一

初识雅思口语

一、雅思口语考试流程

Parts (11-14 minutes)	Contents	Topics
I.D. check (25 to 30 seconds)	Introduction	4 questions
Part 1 (4 to 5 minutes)	Introduction and Interview on Familiar Topics	**Topic 1** – about 4 questions **Topic 2** – about 4 questions **Topic 3** – about 4 questions
Part 2 (3 to 4 minutes)	Individual Long Turn	1 minute of thinking time **Topic 4** – 1 to 2 minute monologue (Possibly) 1 or 2 wrap-up questions
Part 3 (4 to 5 minutes)	Two-Way Discussion	**Topic 5** – about 4 or 5 questions **Topic 6** – about 4 or 5 questions

I.D. Check: Introduction

考官会主动跟考生打招呼并自我介绍，然后用简单问题询问考生身份，目的是要确认身份，这部分主要只是起热身作用。考官一旦打开录音装置，口语考试就已经开始，考生的所有答案都将给考官留下第一印象或者说会影响到整体印象分。

通常这部分有四个固定的问题，持续时间不会超过 30 秒。这些问题分别是：

1. Good morning/afternoon. My name is ______. Can you tell me your full name, please? (Could you tell me your full name, please?/Please tell me your name.)
2. What shall I call you? (What can I call you?/What should I call you?)
3. Can you tell me where you're from? (Could you tell me where you're from?/Where are you from?)
4. Can I see your identification, please? (Could I see your identification, please?/May I see your identification, please?)

Part 1 Introduction and Interview on Familiar Topics

1. 22 秒左右的回答时间

检查完 ID，考官将介绍第一个话题，并围绕这个话题问几个小问题。一般情况下，第一个话题是 your home (house or hometown)或者是 your work / studies。随后考官还会围绕两个话题问一些简单问题。第一部分的考试主要涉及日常生活、学习和工作。一般情况下，每个话题会有 4 个小问题，也就是说第一部分会有 12 个小问题。当然并不绝对，问题的多少也取决于考生答案的长短。因为整个第一部分的时间是 4～5 分钟。大致估算，如果考官问一个问题要花 2 秒钟，那么考生回答每个问题的时间应该在 22 秒左右。因此，这一部分的制胜秘诀是尽可能地多说。当然，也不要将背诵好的长篇大论拿出来，否则一旦被看出，考官就会换题，因为雅思口语考试考核的是考生的口语运用能力，而不是背诵能力。

2. 保持口语的惯性

在回答这部分问题的时候，考生要保持口语的“惯性”，也就是说要滔滔不绝。与考官的问答对话间不要有太多的沉默，要尽可能多地给考官信息，特别是对 yes/no 的问题，千万不要用一个词或一个句子回答，一定要有所发挥。学会如何“调侃”非常重要，给考官一个流畅的感觉同样很重要。而且节奏也十分关键，一定不要慢条斯理，而要有一种紧凑感，问和答之间要快！

3. 学会迂回

考官不会对考生的答案给出任何评价，会用分数来体现。因而考生不要向考官询问他们对你的看法，当然自己也要做到扬长避短。一般情况下，不要暴露自己的词汇不足，不要直接询问某个词汇是什么意思。如果有不太确定的地方要用迂回的方式来询问，比如：“I am not sure, do you mean I should tell you ...” 要比直接问 “What does ... mean?” 要好得多。要特别提醒考生的是，如果不确定考官的问题，不要装懂，因为如果不懂装懂就会答非所问，这样会对分数有很大的影响。考生应该用交际策略弄清楚考官的问题，这也是交际能力或者说口语能力的一种体现。当然，不确定的问题太多也会影响分数。

4. 要有日常话题的口语基本功

第一部分是考核考生是否能谈论日常生活的所有话题，会有一定广度，考生在准备考试的时候应该就日常话题和别人用英语交流，实实在在地提高自己的英语口语基本功。在第一部分结束的时候，考官会提示你将要进行第二部分的考试。

Part 2 Individual Long Turn

第二部分开始的时候，考官会对你说：“I’m now going to give you a topic and I’d like you to talk about that topic for one to two minutes. Before you start to talk, you’ll have one minute to think about what you’re going to say. You can make notes if you wish on this paper. Do you understand?” 同时，考官会给你一张卡片，上面有一个题目，如：

> Describe a website you often use.
> You should say:
> what kind of website it is
> how you find it
> what it is about
> and explain why you like it.

1. 关键的一分钟

接过卡片，考生就可以准备考试了。考生有一分钟的时间准备。这一分钟非常重要，考生要好好利用。要迅速读题，并开始打腹稿，看对于这个话题有哪些方面可以说，该先说什么、再说什么。这些都需要在考前进行一定的训练。在考试的时候，考官为考生准备了一张白纸和一只铅笔，考生可以在白纸上写提纲，一分钟后可以看着提纲来说。

2. 恰到好处的2分钟

在一分钟准备时间结束的时候，考官会问你："Can you start speaking now, please?" (Please start speaking now.) 同时会告诉你有1～2分钟的时间来描述。所以，考生一定要好好把握时间。不要太仓促结束，否则会因长度不够或者语言样本不够，导致考官无从打分，或者不能给你高分。当然，也不要作太多的铺垫，考官让你结束的时候你还没有进入正题也是不可以的，所以，恰到好处非常重要。考生最好让自己的描述成为一个整体，也就是说将原稿写下来，是一篇完整的小短文最好。

3. 独白要洪亮、清晰

在第二部分，考生在说话的时候，考官不会打断你，即便是在没有听见或没有听清的情况下，所以这一部分又叫独白。考生要确定自己说话的时候声音够洪亮、吐词够清晰。考生说完可以用"That's all, thank you."来告知考官你的陈述结束，或者考官会在时间到的时候让你停止。

很多时候，在第二部分结束的时候，考官会根据考生的陈述追问1～2个小问题。问题一般不会太难，考生也不必作太长的回答。考官对考生的答案不太清楚或者感兴趣的时候，才会追问。这同时也暗示考生，第二部分即将结束，要进入第三部分的考试。

4. 话题范围

第二部分的考试话题范围非常广，形式也多种多样，但主要的出题范围是：People, Things, Places, Everyday Activities, Experiences, and Future plans or Speculation about the Future. 一般情况下，这些问题都和考生自己的生活直接相关，所以考生要回答得具体一些，结合自己的生活体验来回答，不要大而化之、泛泛而谈。

5. keep speaking 很关键

第二部分考核深度，即考生是否能对一个话题进行有一定深度的发言。难度自然比第一部分大。这一部分的关键是要keep speaking。1分钟以下的答案会给整体分带来非常大的影响。所以，在备考的时候要练习长度。很多考生都有30秒的"瓶颈"问题，即对第二部分话题只能说到30秒左右，之后就要开始"挤牙膏"了，想一句说一句，并且每说一句都要想下面该说什么，导致流畅不够，从而影响最后得分。

要提醒考生的是：如果考官没有叫停就结束，考生一定要用"Well, that's all I have to say."之类的语言提醒考官你已经说完，不要说完就停着，否则考官会认为你是说不下去了。第二部分的话题不是可选的，也就是说考官给出任何一个卡片，考生都不能要求更换。如果提出要求更换，考官也不会换，而且考官会知道考生不能对任何话题进行谈论，这样会影响考试分数。

还要注意的是，第二部分虽然是一个人的独白，但不要给出太正式的“演讲”式答案。要求语言自然，是要考生对着考官来介绍或者描述所给出的话题，如果太正式就有背诵之嫌了。

Part 3 Two-Way Discussion

第二部分结束后，考官会说：“We've been talking about (Topic 4) and now I'd like to ask you a few more general questions related to (this topic).”从问法上看，第三部分和第一部分相似，和第二部分的话题相关，但更难、更概括、更抽象、也更有深度。问题也不一定是来自题库，考官实时根据考生第二部分的描述进行提问，所以这一部分又叫讨论。考官让考生进一步解释说明考生在第二部分提到的相关问题，或者提出一个与考生不一样的论点，要求考生阐述或答辩等。

如果时间允许，或者考官觉得第二部分的话题已经没有必要再讨论，考官会引出其他与第二部分相关的话题来和考生进行讨论。第三部分会有大概 8 到 10 个问题，当然，问题多少同样取决于考生的答案长度和深度。

1. 常考的话题和概念

总体而言，第一、二部分话题主要关注的是考生本人，而第三部分的话题则更多地关注社会、国家或者政府等更普遍的问题。第三部分常考的话题和概念有： Attitudes and Values，Personal Qualities，Psychology (people's motives and thoughts)，Information and Communication，Society，Change (both cause and effect)，and Education 等。而且，这些问题还会被结合在一起来考。也就是从这些层面提出更具体的问题。从语言功能上讲，第三部分考官经常让考生：give information，speculate，suggest，compare & contrast, explain，give opinion and reasons，justifying or defending opinion 等。

2. 高分的关键

如果考生对第三部分的问题不是很确定，考官会换一种方式再问一遍。但是要提醒的是，第三部分是讨论，所以考生最好不要只是回答问题，要参与讨论，而且讨论要真实、要激烈，可以引经据典，也可以提出佐证。总之，要在这一部分充分体现自己的语言功底，以获得良好印象，从而得到高分。

二、雅思口语评分标准（IELTS Speaking Test Grading Criteria）

雅思口语的评分标准有四个：流畅连贯（Fluency and Coherence）、词汇（Lexical Resource）、语法（Grammatical Range and Accuracy）和语音（Pronunciation）。其每个级别的具体要求如下：

Band	Fluency and coherence	Lexical resource	Grammatical range and accuracy	Pronunciation
9	• speaks fluently with only rare repetition or self-correction; any hesitation is content-related rather than to find words or grammar • speaks coherently with fully appropriate cohesive features • develops topics fully and appropriately	• uses vocabulary with full flexibility and precision in all topics • uses idiomatic language naturally and accurately	• uses a full range of structures naturally and appropriately • produces consistently accurate structures apart from “slips” characteristic of native speaker speech	• uses a full range of pronunciation features with precision and subtlety • sustains flexible use of features throughout • is effortless to understand

（续）

Band	Fluency and coherence	Lexical resource	Grammatical range and accuracy	Pronunciation
8	• speaks fluently with only occasional repetition or self-correction; hesitation is usually content-related and only rarely to search for language • develops topics coherently and appropriately	• uses a wide vocabulary resource readily and flexibly to convey precise meaning • uses less common and idiomatic vocabulary skillfully with occasional inaccuracies • uses paraphrase effectively as required	• uses a wide range of structures flexibly • produces a majority of error-free sentences with only very occasional inappropriacies or basic/non-systematic errors	• uses a wide range of pronunciation features • sustains flexible use of features,with only occasional lapses • is easy to understand throughout; L1 accent has minimal effect on intelligibility
7	• speaks at length without noticeable effort or loss of coherence • uses a range of connectives and discourse markers with some flexibility • may demonstrate language-related hesitation at times, or some repetition and/or self-correction.	• uses vocabulary resource flexibly to discuss a variety of topics • uses some less common and idiomatic vocabulary and shows some awareness of style and collocation with some inappropriate choices • uses paraphrase effectively	• uses a range of complex structures with some flexibility • frequently produces error-free sentences, though some grammatical mistakes persist	• shows all the positive features of Band 6 and some, but not all, of the positive features of Band 8
6	• is willing to speak at length, though may lose coherence at times due to occasional repetition, self-correction or hesitation • uses a range of connectives and discourse markers but not always appropriately	• has a wide enough vocabulary to discuss topics at length and make meaning clear in spite of inappropriacies • generally paraphrases successfully	• uses a mix of simple and complex structures, but with limited flexibility • may make frequent mistakes with complex structures, though these rarely cause comprehension problems	• uses a range of pronunciation features with mixed control • shows some effective use of features but this is not sustained • can generally be understood throughout, though mispronunciation of individual words or sounds reduces clarity at times
5	• usually maintains flow of speech but uses repetition, self-correction and/or slow speech to keep going • may overuse certain connectives and discourse markers • produces simple speech fluently, but more complex communication causes fluency problems	• manages to talk about familiar and unfamiliar topics but uses vocabulary with limited flexibility • attempts to paraphrase but with mixed success	• produces basic sentence forms with reasonable accuracy • uses a limited range of more complex structures, but these usually contain errors and may cause some comprehension problems	• shows all the positive features of Band 4 and some, but not all, of the positive features of Band 6

（续）

Band	Fluency and coherence	Lexical resource	Grammatical range and accuracy	Pronunciation
4	• cannot respond without noticeable pauses and may speak slowly, with frequent repetition and self-correction • links basic sentences but with repetitious use of simple connectives and some breakdowns in coherence	• is able to talk about familiar topics but can only convey basic meaning on unfamiliar topics and makes frequent errors in word choice • rarely attempts paraphrase	• produces basic sentence forms and some correct simple sentences but subordinate structures are rare • errors are frequent and may lead to misunderstanding	• uses a limited range of pronunciation features • attempts to control features but lapses are frequent • mispronunciations are frequent and cause some difficulty for the listener
3	• speaks with long pauses • has limited ability to link simple sentences • gives only simple responses and is frequently unable to convey basic message	• uses simple vocabulary to convey personal information • has insufficient vocabulary for less familiar topics	• attempts basic sentence forms but with limited success, or relies on apparently memorised utterances • makes numerous errors except in memorised expressions	• shows some of the features of Band 2 and some, but not all, of the positive features of Band 4
2	• pauses lengthily before most words • little communication possible	• only produces isolated words or memorised utterances	• cannot produce basic sentence forms	• speech is often unintelligible
1	no communication possible no rateable language			
0	does not attend			

得分	流利度与连贯性	词汇资源	语法结构的范围和准确性	发音
9	发言时极少有重复或自我更正，偶尔的停顿也是由于在思考内容，而非搜寻合适的词汇和语法 发言连贯，语言中上下文流畅，联系自然而充分 全面而得体地围绕话题展开发言	面对任何话题都能灵活、准确地使用词汇 自然、准确地使用习语	自然、准确地使用多样语法结构 语法结构的使用自始至终保持准确，虽然偶尔犯一些英语为母语者也会犯的“口误”	能完全精确地发出所有英语语音 能灵活使用英语发音 不对听者造成任何理解上的困难
8	发言时很少有重复或自我更正，偶尔的停顿也多是由于在思考内容，极少情况下是为了搜寻合适的语言 连贯而得体地围绕话题展开发言	能自然、灵活地使用多样词汇来准确表达思想 能巧妙使用较不常见单词和习语，尽管偶尔有不准确 能按要求有效使用同一语言的其他表达方式	灵活使用多种结构 大部分语句无误，极偶尔情况下出现错误，或个别简单错误	使用多种语音手段来有效达意 能灵活使用多种语音手段，但偶尔有错 自始至终易于理解，母语语音对英语的影响极小

（续）

得分	流利度与连贯性	词汇资源	语法结构的范围和准确性	发音
7	能充分展开，且不会有刻意思考的痕迹，没有语言上的不连贯 能较灵活地使用连接词或语言中的信号词 有时会出现由于语言水平而造成的重复或自我更正	能灵活使用词汇讨论多种话题 能使用较不常见单词和习语，对语体和搭配有所了解，尽管有时不准确 能有效使用同一语言的其他表达方式	较灵活地使用多种复杂结构 多数语句无误，但有些错误一直存在	具备 6 分的所有要求，但不完全具备 8 分的发音要求
6	有充分交流的意识，但有时由于重复、自我更正或停顿而导致不连贯 能使用连接词或语言中的信号词，尽管有时不准确	有足够的词汇来充分讨论话题，清晰达意，尽管有时不准确 大致可以使用同一语言的其他表达方式	能使用简单和复杂结构，但缺乏灵活性 复杂结构经常出现错误，尽管这些错误很少导致交流障碍	能使用较多英语发音手段 一般能有效使用英语发音方法 自始至终可以被理解，尽管发音错误偶尔会为听者带来一点费解
5	通常能维持语流，但需要通过重复、自我更正或放慢语速才能实现流畅 可能会过多使用某些连接词或语言中的信号词 能流畅表达简单语言，复杂语言会导致语言不畅	能讨论熟悉或不熟悉的话题，但词汇使用缺乏灵活性 尝试使用同一语言的其他表达方式，但未必都能成功	能使用基本的句子结构，且使用基本正确 复杂结构的使用有限，且通常包含错误，有时导致交流障碍	具备 4 分所有的发音要求，但不完全具备 6 分的发音要求
4	回答时有明显停顿，语速可能较慢，时常有重复、自我更正 能把基本句连接起来，但重复使用某些简单连接词，语意上多有不连贯之处	能讨论熟悉话题，对于不熟悉话题只能表达意思，词汇的选择上时常犯错 很少尝试使用同一语言的其他表达方式	能使用基本的句子结构或正确的简单句，但从句结构很少见 错误频繁，可能导致误解	可以发出英语中某些语音 尝试发出英语中的语音，但经常不准确 经常发错音，给听者带来严重理解困难
3	发言时停顿过长 连接简单句的能力有限 只给简单答复，时常难以表达基本想法	使用简单语言表达个人信息 遇到较不熟悉的话题词汇匮乏	尝试使用简单句子结构，但不成功，或明显背诵事先准备的语言 表达中错误很多（背过的表达除外）	具备 2 分的要求，但不完全具备 4 分的要求
2	说大多数词前都要长时间地思考停顿 最简单基本的交流	只能说只言片语或事先背过的语言	不能使用基本的句子形式	语言经常无法识别
1	无法交流，语言无法评估			
0	缺席考试			

考官根据考生的考场表现，分别给出四个具体的分数，并算出平均分，其平均分就是考生的最后得分。计算方式如下：

Marking Criteria	Band	Band	Band
Fluency and Coherence	5	6	7
Lexical Resource	4	5	7
Grammatical Range and Accuracy	5	6	8
Pronunciation	5	5	7
Final Band (Average Score)	19/4 = 4.75 = **Band 4.5**	22/4 = 5.5 = **Band 5.5**	29/4 = 7.25 = **Band 7.0**

三、雅思口语评分标准深度解析

究竟该如何在口语考试中拿高分，各个评分标准又分别指什么呢？下面我们逐一进行详细的讲解。

（一）保证 Fluency and Coherence 的 2 个关键因素

Fluency and Coherence refers to the ability to talk with normal levels of continuity, rate and effort and to link ideas and language together to form coherent, connected speech.

The key indicators of **fluency** are speech rate and speech continuity.

The key indicators of **coherence** are logical sequencing of sentences, clear marking of stages in a discussion, narration or argument, and the use of cohesive devices (e.g. connectors, pronouns and conjunctions) within and between sentences.

1. 控制语速

具体而言，流畅更直观地讲就是要注意语速。但并非越快越好。每个人有不同的语速，所谓流畅也就是用自己的正常语速回答问题。可以尝试说快点，但前提是不要影响语音语调的准确性。连贯就是要求停顿不要太多、太久。当问题提出后，如果 5 秒以内还不给答案，考官会默认为你不会回答该题，因而会换题，或者直接进入下一个话题。这样自然会影响考生得分，为了避免这种情况，考生可以用一些填充词，如: Well，hm，let me see，actually，you know 等填充词来确保流畅，至少让考官先不要换题。

2. 增加连词的使用

确保连贯的另一个关键性因素就是要注意使用连词。由于中文不用太多连词，所以中国人没有注意去使用连词，而英语的逻辑往往是靠连接词来实现的。如果不用，会让外国考官觉得不自然。比如下面两个自我介绍：“I am a teacher, I teach English, I like teaching, my students are very active in the class, I feel happy to be with my students.”/“I am a teacher, **and** I teach english, I like teaching, **because** my students are very active in my class, **so** I feel happy to be with them.” 简单三个连词的使用，就把一些罗列堆积的句子变成了一段话。也就更显得自然连贯了。

当然连贯还要求前后时态一致，内容不冲突。能达到这个评分标准，考生的分数必将在5分以上。

（二）查出误区，理解 Lexical Resource 的真实涵义

Lexical Resource refers to the range of vocabulary the candidate can use and the precision with which meanings and attitudes can be expressed.

The key indicators are the **variety** of words used, the **adequacy** and **appropriateness** of the words used and the ability to communicate (get round a vocabulary gap by using other words) with or without noticeable hesitation.

1. 正确理解雅思口语词汇

对于词汇，广大中国学员有一个理解上的误区，觉得自己英语不好就是词汇量不够。经常有人说，我的口语不好，因为我的词汇量太少。其实，这只说对了一半。词汇量是会对一个外语学习者的语言水平尤其是口语水平产生很大的影响，但是，口语不好，不能全归咎于词汇量不够。其实，口语中所用的都是高频词汇，也就是说口语对词汇量的要求不是很高。要知道朗文词典的解释词汇才 2000 个，也就是说它用 2000 词汇解释了所有词汇，可见这 2000 词汇的表达力有多强。事实上，掌握 4000 个单词，就能用英语谈论生活中的所有话题。但是，这 4000 词汇必须是积极词汇（active vocabulary），也就是说不能只是在阅读和听力中能识别，还必须能用。所以对雅思口语词汇的储备，考生通过反复练习自己已经掌握的高频词汇就可以了。

2. 善用多个词表达

当然，在考试的时候还有一些技巧。比如：不能多次重复使用同一词，lexical resource 的真实涵义是指能用多个词表达同样一个概念。反复使用同一个词，证明考生的词汇量不足。另外，用词要具体，不要太概括。如 good，beautiful，delicious 要尽可能少用，应该换成更具体的形容词。特别要注意的是，有很多考生学习词汇的方式不对，主要是通过背诵单词表来记忆单词，这样必然导致口语的翻译腔，甚至出现大量的中式英语，这会对词汇得分起很大的负面作用。如：“It is good to my body health.” 就是典型的中式英语，正确的应该是：“It is good for my health.”

（三）应对 Grammatical Range and Accuracy 有窍门

Grammatical Range and Accuracy refers to the range and the accurate and appropriate use of the candidate’s grammatical resource.

The key indicators of grammatical range are the length and complexity of the spoken sentences, the appropriate use of subordinate clauses, and the range of sentence structures, especially to move elements around for information focus.

The key indicators of grammatical accuracy are the number of grammatical errors in a given amount of speech and the communicative effect of error.

1. 回避低级语法错误

口语考试的最大好处是一切由考生说了算。虽然考生不能选择话题，但是考生可以选择用什么语言来答题。也就说，考生有机会扬长避短，选择自己确信是正确的句子来回答问题。比如，有的考生对“虚拟语气”和部分“从句”拿不准，在口语中就可以选择不用。但是，考生可以回避高难度的语法，对很多基础语法却是没有办法回避的。比如：“he/she 混淆”、“时态错误”、“名词复数，动词三单”使用错误、“形容词修饰名词，副词修饰动词”的修饰关系把握不准等。这些语法错误属于低级语法错误。出现这些错误会给考官留下极其不好的印象。在本族语使用者看来，如果这些语法都错，可见语法非常不好。其实，中国学员往往就是在这些小问题上出错。不是考生不知道语法规则，而是在说话的时候更多地在关注说什么，不知不觉中就会出现这些错误。所以，考生一定要有意识地在口语中训练，尽量不要出现这些错误。

2. 不要反复用同一个句型

语法的范围主要是指考生能用的句型结构的多样性。所以考生要特别注意不要反复使用同一个句型来回答问题，要有意识地不断更换句型，将简单句和复杂句穿插使用。让语言听起来不至于枯燥，也不要因为句型而影响考官对答案的理解。

（四）不要害怕你的 Pronunciation

Pronunciation refers to the ability to produce comprehensible speech to fulfill the speaking test requirements. The key indicators will be the amount of strain caused to the listener, the amount of the speech which is unintelligible and the notice ability of L1 influence.

很多考生都觉得自己的发音不准，其实大可不必着急。比较而言，中国人的外语学习天赋还是很强的。在把英语当外语学习的国家里，中国人的发音是很准确的。雅思口语对发音的要求也不是很苛刻，只要让考官听懂无障碍就可以了。

具体地讲，要发准每个音素、每个单词，特别要注意 th 的发音，n/l 的发音，v/w 的发音等；要恰当使用连读、弱读、失去爆破；要准确使用重音和语调。

星期二 感受雅思口语

星期一我们全面了解了雅思口语考试，星期二我们来深度学习一套雅思口语真题。通过解答这套真题，考生可以亲自感受一下考试流程和具体的评分标准。

一、找个“考官”摸摸底

首先，请找一个“考官”考一考你自己，或者你自问自答，将整个流程录音，并给自己打一个分数，看你现在能得几分？

The Introduction (25 to 30 seconds)

1. Good morning. My name is… Can you tell me your full name, please?
2. What shall I call you?
3. Can you tell me where you're from?
4. Can I see your identification, please?

Part 1 (4 to 5 minutes)

Topic 1 Television

1. Do you like watching television?
2. How much time (per day/per week etc.) do you spend watching television?
3. What programs do you like to watch?
4. What benefits can people get from watching foreign TV programs?

Topic 2 Dance

1. Do you like dancing?
2. What kind of dancing is popular in China?
3. When do people dance?
4. What do you think people can benefit from dancing?

Topic 3 Ambitions

1. What are your ambitions?
2. Do you think you can realize them?
3. What difficulties do you think you might have?

4. Do you think it is good to be ambitious?

Part 2 (3 to 4 minutes)

Topic 4

Describe a website you often use. You should say: what kind of website it is how you find it what it is about and explain why you like it.

wrap-up questions:

1. Do Chinese people often use that site?
2. Have you told anybody else about this website?

Part 3 (4 to 5 minutes)

Topic 5 The (dis)advantages of the Internet

1. What convenience has Internet bring to people's life?
2. Do you think the government should control the Internet?
3. Many people read online, do you think the Internet will take the place of books in the future?
4. Do you think elder people can benefit the same from the Internet?

Topic 6 The Internet in education

1. In China, is the Internet used much in schools or colleges/universities?
2. Is the Internet very useful for teaching purposes?
3. What are the benefits of using the Internet in schools?
4. Do you prefer using the Internet to find information or do you prefer using a library?

Marking criteria	Band
Fluency and Coherence	
Lexical Resource	
Grammatical Range and Accuracy	
Pronunciation	
Final Band (Average Score)	

二、你探到底了吗？

你给自己打了多少分？你期待着考多少分呢？你对自己的评分客观准确吗？下面有两位同学的答案，他们的口语得分分别是 5 分和 8 分。仔细对比你和两位同学的三套答案，深度领悟雅思口语评分标准。

下面是雅思口语5分的答案。考官评语是：

“能比较流畅地用简单语言回答问题，但使用复杂语言不够，而且不是很准确。词汇使用灵活性不是很强。语言连贯性不够，且经常有重复和自我更正。语言错误较多。发音基本能理解。”

The Introduction (25 to 30 seconds)

1. Good morning. My name is George. Can you tell me your full name, please?

— Good morning. My name is Tan Chang.

2. What shall I call you?

— You should call me Nicole. This is my English name.

3. Can you tell me where you're from?

— I was born and brought up in Hubei Province.

4. Can I see your identification, please?

— Sure!

Part 1 (4 to 5 minutes)

Topic 1 Television

1. Do you like watching television?

— Yes, I do. I like it very much.

2. How much time (per day/per week etc.) do you spend watching television?

— Well, I spend about two hours a day on TV.

3. What programs do you like to watch?

— I like watching almost every kind of TV programs, but my favorite is sports news.

4. What benefits can people get from watching foreign TV programs?

— By watching TV, we can get the latest news and it is the cheapest entertainment.

Topic 2 Dance

1. Do you like dancing?

— Honestly speaking, I don't like dancing, but sometimes I dance with my friends.

2. What kind of dancing is popular in China?

— Nowadays, more and more people like dancing hip hop, I think the main reason is that hip hop can help release people's stress. Also, people share happiness as well as sorrow with each other.

3. When do people dance?

— Normally, people will dance after dinner, because people work in the daytime and then take the evening off to relax and enjoy themselves.

4. What do you think people can benefit from dancing?

— Well, I think it is a very good way to keep fit, and also a good way to make friends.

Topic 3 Ambitions

1. What are your ambitions?

— Well, I have many ambitions, but first of all, I want to have my own company.

2. Do you think you can realize them?

— Yes, nothing is impossible if I want to do it.

3. What difficulties do you think you might have?

— You know it is not easy, first I need a great amount of money, and survive in the competition.

4. Do you think it is good to be ambitious?

— Certainly, it can keep me positive and it is good to have dreams.

Part 2 (3 to 4 minutes)

Topic 4

Describe a website you often use You should say: what kind of website it is how you find it what it is about and explain why you like it.

—Honestly speaking, I don't often surf the Internet due to the busy schedule of my study. But I think I do have adequate knowledge to talk about it since, luckily for me, I've found a website I often use it. I am sure everybody knows taobao, an e-shopping web. And I have known it for a long time. In fact, it contains so many goods, and I found it especially useful for me, as I mentioned above, I study hard and have no time to go shopping, so I buy all the clothes and books I need on taobao.com, besides, you can also find many fashion news on net. It can tell you how to wear and how to make you more beautiful. And I hope that you can also try it out and I am sure you won't be disappointed.

wrap-up questions:

1. Do Chinese people often use that site?

— Yes, as society has entered the information age and commercialization is sweeping across the world, Internets bring many benefits and conveniences to people.

2. Have you told anybody else about this website?

— Yes, I always share good things with my friends.

Part 3 (4 to 5 minutes)

Topic 5 The (dis)advantages of the Internet

1. What convenience has Internet bring to people's life?

— The Internet has brought many conveniences to our life. For example, we shop online, so that we don't have to waste time going shopping.

2. Do you think the government should control the Internet?

— Yes, I think so. Because there is much information which is very negative, such as violence and porn which are very bad to children.

3. Many people read online, do you think the Internet will take the place of books in the future?

— I don't think so. I think many people still like reading books, because it is healthier. Computers are very bad to our eyes.

4. Do you think elder people can benefit the same from the Internet?

— No, I don't think so. Because many elder people cannot use computer, so they actually can not benefit from the Internet.

Topic 6 The Internet in education

1. In China, is the Internet used much in schools or colleges/universities?

— Yes, computers and networks now are widely used in universities; students can use it to have classes.

2. Is the Internet very useful for teaching purposes?

— Sure. Because the Internet has a variety of knowledge, such as history, students can see the history pictures from the Internet rather than just read them from books.

3. What are the benefits of using the internet in schools?

— It makes high quality of education. Teachers can use many pictures to show textbook. This can improve students' interest.

4. Do you prefer using the Internet to find information or do you prefer using a library?

— From my part, I prefer using the Internet to find information. For example, I am sure everybody knows Google, a searching engine; I usually search some background information on the related subject, such as the European history and the furniture items.

下面是雅思口语 8 分的答案。考官评语是：
“能流畅回答所有问题，词汇使用灵活，句型多样，错误极少。”

The Introduction (25 to 30 seconds)

1. Good morning. My name is George. Can you tell me your full name, please?

— Good morning. My full name is Zhan Shengqi, Z-H-A-N, Zhan is my family name.

2. **What shall I call you?**

— Please just call me Ross, which is my English name.

3. **Can you tell me where you're from?**

— I come from the city of Wuxi in Jiangsu Province, which is very close to Shanghai.

4. **Can I see your identification, please?**

— Sure, here it is!

Part 1 (4 to 5 minutes)

Topic 1 Television

1. **Do you like watching television?**

— Yes, I do. Watching television is a way of relaxation to me. Generally speaking, I watch news program such as domestic news and world news. It's quite informative.

2. **How much time (per day/per week etc.) do you spend watching television?**

— Well, I watch about two hours on a daily basis. On weekends, especially on Friday and Saturday nights, I spend more hours in watching television because I don't have to get up early on the next mornings.

3. **What programs do you like to watch?**

— There are several types of programs I like to watch. For example, news programs, chat shows, variety shows as well as soaps. Among these, my favorite ones are news programs and chat shows.

4. **What benefits can people get from watching foreign TV programs?**

— Obviously, people can learn foreign culture as these kinds of TV Programs present the way of life of people of different cultures. Ideally, people's vision can be broadened and hopefully they can be open and understanding and tolerant to people from other cultures.

Topic 2 Dance

1. **Do you like dancing?**

— Not really, I am a quiet man; I much prefer to stay alone and watch a movie or something.

2. **What kind of dancing is popular in China?**

— Frankly speaking, I have no idea, but I have seen many classmates dancing hip hop, because they like the music played for the dancing, and social dancing is always very popular in China.

3. **When do people dance?**

— I think it depends, for example, elder people often get up early and dance in the parks, while young people may dance in the bars in the evening. And many people dance at parties.

4. **What do you think people can benefit from dancing?**

— Well, I think people can benefit a lot from dancing. First of all, it is a very good way to relax, by dancing, mang people forget all the unhappiness they have in their work or life. In addition, dancing is a good way to make friends.

Topic 3 Ambitions

1. **What are your ambitions?**

— Well, I have many ambitions. First of all, I want to have my PH.D degree in Oxford University, then I want to come back to China and have my ideal job, with several years of working experience, I would like to set up my own company.

2. **Do you think you can realize them?**

— Sure, I am very perseverant and hard-working. What I am studying now will be very helpful for my ambitions, and I have many relatives work in this field, so I can get enough help if I want to set up my own company. You know in China, personal connections are very important to be successful.

3. **What difficulties do you think you might have?**

— Well, having a good job may not be hard, but to set up my own business and be successful is another story. First of all, I will have to be rich, and I have to know the field very well. What's more, I need many people to help me.

4. **Do you think it is good to be ambitious?**

— Personally, I think so, because being ambitions may make me more hardworking. Therefore, I can succeed more.

Part 2 (3 to 4 minutes)

Topic 4

Describe a website you often use. You should say: what kind of website it is how you find it what it is about and explain why you like it.

I would like to describe a website that I often use, which is called www.goodenglish.com.cn. It is a personal English website. I got the website from a friend. You know I want to go to UK to further my education, so I have to learn English well. Once in an English class, I was talking with a friend about the resources I can use for my English learning, he recommended this website to me.

I tried it immediately when I got home and was deeply attracted by this website, because it got so many resources for my English learning, I can learn English vocabulary and grammar on it, I can also find writing samples to learn from, so I have been using it since I got the website, owing to which my English has been improved greatly.

I am very grateful to my friend and the owner of the website, I think the owner must be a very great guy, because he shares his information with unknown people for free.

wrap-up questions:

1. Do Chinese people often use that site?

— Well, I don't think so, because it is a very small website and there is no advertisement for it, because it is non-beneficial.

2. Have you told anybody else about this website?

— Yes, I told everybody I know that is learning English.

Part3 (4 to 5 minutes)

Topic 5 The (dis) advantages of the Internet

1. What convenience has Internet bring to people's life?

— I think the Internet has changed our life in every aspect, it is almost impossible for me to name all of the conveniences it has brought to our life. Let me take sharing information as an example, we can get all the information we need for our study and work, and don't have to spend days searching in the library. And we can share information with people without considering where they are.

2. Do you think the government should control the Internet?

— I would say yes, because right now, the Internet is kind of out of control. As a result, the Internet became a platform for some bad people, such as criminals. It is said that there are too much violence and porn on the Internet, which may have very bad influence on children.

3. Many people read online, do you think the internet will take the place of books in the future?

— Well, as far as I know it is impossible. Take me for example; I like reading, which is actually one of my hobbies. Just imagine, in the afternoon, I sit on my balcony, enjoying the sunshine, tasty tea, and an interesting book. That is life, which cannot be replaced by any media or any entertainment. So, it is not what you can read, but how you read. I mean, the Internet may provide everything you want to read, but it is always a computer, not a book.

4. Do you think elder people can benefit the same from the Internet?

— No, definitely not. Because Internet has only been widely used in the last decade, which means the elder people did not learn computer when they were young, and because of their education background, it is rather hard for them to learn now. If they cannot use computers even, how can they benefit from it?

Topic 6 The Internet in education

1. In China, is the Internet used much in schools or colleges/universities?

— Yes, it is very widely used actually, especially in the universities. Almost every classroom is computerized with Internet access. And the students can surf online in their dorms as well. What's more, the professors often use the Internet in both preparing classes and lecturing.

2. Is the Internet very useful for teaching purposes?

— Sure, you know my uncle is a university professor. He used Internet a lot. Actually he relies on the Internet a lot. You know he prepares lectures by using Internet, he collects assignments online. So he is basically home-based. I think there are many teachers like him.

3. What are the benefits of using the Internet in schools?

— I guess there are many benefits for both teachers and students. First of all, it can help to make sure the knowledge the students learn is the most updated, and is very convenient and economical for teachers and students to communicate online. Finally, the students and teachers can use the information that is not available in their own universities.

4. Do you prefer using the Internet to find information or do you prefer using a library?

— I much prefer using the Internet, because I don't have to commute to a library, and I only need to move my fingers and I can get everything I need. Why should I bother to use a library?

星期三

雅思口语答题的13个TIPS

雅思口语考试有一些基本原则，考生必须牢记在心，并且在准备和练习的阶段不断练习，以达到炉火纯青的状态。这样，在考试的时候就可以考出应该有的甚至是比自己实际水平还高的分数。

电影是雅思口语考试非常高频的话题，曾经在第1、2、3部分多次考过。所以对于这个话题必须要有充足的准备。既要有广度，即有关电影的方方面面都要能谈；也要有深度，即对电影进行深度描写和讨论。今天我们就来深度学习这个话题。从第1、2、3部分充分准备这个话题，并举一反三，深入学习和领会雅思口语考试的技巧和获得高分的策略。

一、与film有关的问题

Part 1

1. Do you like watching films?
2. What types of films do you like and what types of films do you dislike?
3. What kind of films did you like to watch when you were a child?
4. Do you prefer to watch films at home or in a cinema? (Why?)

Part 2

Describe a film you (recently) enjoyed watching.
You should say:
　　what type of film it was
　　where you watched this film
　　what the film was about
and explain why you enjoyed this film.

Part 3

1. Do you have any favourite film stars (or actors or actresses)? （*provide information*）
2. Do you and your parents like to watch the same kinds of films? （*comparing*）
3. What sorts of films do you think are unsuitable for children to watch? （*provide information*）
4. Is there any difference between the kinds of films people in China watch today and the kinds of films they watched before (for example, 20～50 years ago)? （*comparing*）
5. In general, do you think films (popular movies) have any educational value? （*give opinions*

and reasons）

6. Do you prefer to watch foreign films or domestically made (Chinese) films? （*contrast*）
7. What are the most common themes of films today? （*provide information*）
8. Have you ever been confused by the difference between the "academic" English you learned in school and the English used in films? (*explaining*)
9. Do you think watching foreign movies in English can help you (or help people) learn English? (*give opinions and reasons*)
10. Can you suggest some ways that the film industry could use to attract a larger audience to their films? (*suggesting*)

二、答题技巧和策略

考官可以通过这个话题考核考生各个方面的能力。第 1 部分考核考生对电影的喜好、电影种类、看电影的场所；第 2 部分描写一部电影；第 3 部分分别考核了：compare & contrast，give information，give opinions & reasons，suggesting，explaining 等。下面我们就针对这些问题一一作答，并同时学习雅思口语考试的技巧策略，以及常见的答题思路。

Part 1

1. Do you like watching films?

周计划提示

TIP 1: 感情不要太平淡

喜好（do you like ...）是一个非常高频的雅思口语考题，第一部分的很多话题都是以这个问题引出的，如："Do you like reading / watching TV / dancing / traveling / surfing the internet / music / flowers / birds / animals? 等。但很多考生受以前英语学习习惯的影响，总是给出最为平淡的答案，如：Do you like flowers？" 很多考生直接答："Yes, I like flowers, I think they are beautiful." 或者是 "No, I don't like flowers." 这样的答案都会让人听起来十分无趣。它既违背了英语不重复动词的原则，也显得句型单一。仔细分析原因，还是考生约束了自己的思维。其实，每个人对一个东西的喜好是非常多样的。考生不妨放开思路，具体一点，表达出自己的细节情感，或许会更真实、更自然、效果也自然更好。如：

- Well, I love flowers, especially the fragrant ones; I often buy some and put them in my bedroom, so as to make my room smell like a garden.
- Not really, actually, I hate flowers, because I am allergic to many flowers. Very often, by passing by the flower shops, I may result in feeling dizzy or even having to go to the hospital.

表达好恶的结构有很多，比如：

I like reading.	I dislike reading.
I enjoy reading.	I don't like reading.
I love reading.	I hate reading.

I am keen on reading.
I am interested in reading.
I fancy reading.
I am fond of reading.
I have crush on reading.
I am crazy about reading.
I am addicted to reading.
I can't live without reading.
Reading is my favorite.
Reading is fun.

I am not interested in reading.
I am sick of reading.
Reading is boring.
Reading is the last thing I would like to do.

在回答这类问题的时候，一定要注意感情色彩。千万不要因为句型和表达法不够而让自己的答案不能表达自己的真实情感。

问题 1 的答案可以非常多样化，如：

—Yes, I do. I watch films every week, I think watching movies is one of the best entertainments.

—Frankly speaking, I am crazy about movies, especially those acted by the most well-known actors and actresses, watching those good-looking people is already very relaxing, without mentioning the complex and touching plots.

—Not really, I am not a movie goer, I think it is kind of time wasting, I have things that are much more meaningful to do.

周计划提示

TIP 2：肢体语言、面部表情和目光接触很重要

肢体语言、面部表情和目光接触都对交流产生非常重要的作用。由于雅思口语考核考生的交际能力，在恰当的时候使用这些非语言的因素，能帮助考生表达自己的意思，从而弥补词汇和语言的不足。比如在第 2 部分描述题中，在对形状和方位的描述时，如果语言不够用，可以用手势结合铅笔和白纸比划，这样就可以把词汇的不足掩盖于无形之中。要求面部表情和所用语言的感情色彩一致，暗示考官你是在用语言说话，而不是在背诵答案。目光的接触更能体现考生的自信和对英语文化的深层理解。西方人比东方人的目光接触多，不敢看对方眼睛会被认为是不真诚的“心虚”或不自信。因此要与考官对视，用眼睛说话，有时候不用说考官也能明白，这样就远比纯语言的交流容易地多。只要考官感觉交流无障碍，那么考生交际能力就得到了足够的体现。

2．**What types of films do you like and what types of films do you dislike?**

3．**What kind of films did you like to watch when you were a child?**

周计划提示

TIP 3：善意的谎言也是必要的

雅思口语考试主要是考语言水平，评分标准不包含内容，考官对这些具体问题的答案内容也不感兴趣。因此，考试的目的是明确的，也是唯一的，即只要有助于拿高分的任何策略和内容都是可取的。不要拘泥于实际情况。况且对很多考生而言，很多问题是没有答案的。但一旦被问到，即便是编造，也要给出答案。因此，这时候的不真实答案最多也就是善意的谎言，考生可以尽管使用。如：当被问到“what kind of sports do you like best?”的时候，中国考生经常跳不出 basketball，football，table tennis，swimming 和 badminton 的圈子。其实体育运动那么多，随便给一个，效果都比这 5 个好，反正考官不会让你现场表演。只要能自圆其说，体现英语口语水平就无可厚非。比如下面的答案是不是就会有趣地多。

- Well, I quite like sports, but my favorite is still boxing, because I am going abroad to further my study, so I have to learn to protect myself. （女生使用这个效果更好）
- Well, quite recently, I have developed my interest in weight lifting, because it can help me to shape my body, I think with more muscles I will be more attractive to girls.

如果实在想说 swimming 也可以，那就建议这么说：“Well, my favorite sports is swimming, especially back stroke swimming, lying on the water, I feel like flying. It is also good to my figure.”至少让考官知道你能表达出具体的一种游泳 (breast stroke，butterfly，freestyle)，这样考官会从词汇角度给你加分。

又如：Do you collect anything? 被过度使用的一个答案是：I collect stamps. 也许这是实话，但是这个实话绝对不会帮你拿雅思口语高分。建议给出更多选项，即便不是真实的。如：

- Well, I collect plastic bottles; I mean the soft drink containers. I have hundreds at home, I put them into different shape, which makes very good decoration for my room.

如果一时间想不起来，那就说考试的时候能看到的东西，如：pencil, shoes, pictures, t-shirt 等。因为考官根本无所谓你到底收藏什么，他们关注的是你如何用英语表达自己的业余爱好。

本话题词汇储备：

Types of Movies

documentary	记录片	comedy	喜剧片
tragedy	悲剧片	horror movie	恐怖片
swordsmen movie	武侠片	action movie	动作片
detective film	侦探片	ethical film	伦理片
western movie	西部片	animation，cartoon（movie）	动画片
science fiction	科幻片	costume play	古装戏
war movie	战争片	disaster movie	灾难片
literary film	文艺片	musicals	音乐片
newsreel	新闻片		

第 3 题的回答可以是：

—I like all kinds of movies, but action movie is my favorite, especially the movies of James Bond, because every movie he acted is very exciting, you know, with very complex plot and very advanced weapons.

周计划提示

TIP 4：恰当地使用幽默

幽默是英语本身的一大特点。很多英语本族语使用者都十分幽默。如果能恰当地使用幽默，必然能给考官留下深刻印象。使用幽默是英语水平的一个很具体的体现，而且幽默可以营造一个轻松的考场氛围，让考官不至于觉得监考是那么痛苦和枯燥。这样给出高分的可能性会大大增加。如："What do you normally do in your spare time?"是经常被问到的一个考题。很多考生都循规蹈矩，非常诚实地给出："In my spare time, I often go to play basket ball/ football with my friends."似乎所有中国考生都无其他事可做。其实，这个题目是最容易体现答案多样性、语言个性和幽默的一个题目。这里给出几个仅供大家参考。

- Well, frankly speaking, I don't have much spare time, cos I have much work to do, but whenever I get some time off, I would go to watch a horror movie with my girlfriend, because she is really crazy about it.
- Well, in my spare time, the only thing that I fancy doing is to chat with my online wife, I have a wife online, we have an e-pet and a house online, we chat a lot online, but we never meet.
- Well you know, I collect teeth of all kinds of animals including human. So I spend a lot of my spare time searching for the teeth in whatever sources available.

第 3 题的回答也可以是：

—Well, my favorite is horror movie, actually I didn't like it before. I found it scaring, and after watching horror movies, I often have nightmares. However, unfortunately, my girl friend loves it very much, and at the very beginning I tried to pretend to be a real man, but gradually, I found it is very relaxing, and after constant screaming, all the pressure I got from work and life is released.

4. **Do you prefer to watch films at home or in a cinema? (Why?)**

—I much prefer to watch a movie in a cinema, because the atmosphere is much better, you know, it is very romantic with the curtains on, and also it can provide the best audio and video effect, which makes watching itself a kind of relaxation without considering the content of the movies.

—Well, as for me, watching movies at home is more comfortable. My father collects DVDs, and he has a collection of more than one thousand, so I can pick up whatever movie I like. What's more, every time, when I stay at home and watch a movie, my mom will cook me very tasty food.

Part 2

Describe a film you (recently) enjoyed watching.
You should say:
    what type of film it was
    where you watched this film
    what the film was about
and explain why you enjoyed this film.

周计划提示

TIP 5：思路很重要

很多考生都有30秒的瓶颈问题，也就是说对任何话题都只能说到30秒左右，之后就是想一句说一句，挤牙膏似的。这必然会影响考试得分。因此，第二部分的答题思路非常重要，这些都应该在复习准备阶段做好充分的准备，对不同类型的考题思路进行整理，并固化下来。在考试的时候，接过卡片，马上在考官给你准备的白纸上写下答题思路。然后好好利用1分钟的准备时间具体地看该说些什么。

比如：描写电影可以从这些方面去说：

- title
- director
- actors and actresses
- plot
- costume
- script
- comment (influence of the movie; audio and video effect etc.)

很多考生经常犯的一个错误是拿着电影就讲述电影中的故事。其实，要想用两分钟的时间把一个电影的故事说清楚不是一件容易的事。而且即便是做到了，也不够。所以，考试的时候应该从更多的侧面去描述这个电影，而情节部分只用简短的几句话带过就可以了。这样做既可以保证两分钟的内容含量没有问题，还可以保证描述全面，让考官觉得耳目一新。

TIP 6：尽可能地多说

有了思路之后，在考试的时候，就要抓住所有时间，尽可能地多说。因为在雅思口语考试中，考生扮演的是说话者的角色，考官的主要任务则是倾听。如果考生说的话太少，考官取样不足，考生成绩肯定不理想。尤其是Part II和Part III，考生的回答必须尽可能完整、充分，对于第二部分的答案如果没说到1分钟，那是非常危险的。即便是Part I的问题，也要尽量避免出现“一句作答”的情况，更不用说用一个词或一个词组来回答了。总之，考生要抓住一切机会和时间说话，给考官一个流畅的感觉，才有希望拿高分。在流畅与精确不能同时兼顾的时候，宁可先保证流畅，偶尔错一点，只要不影响交流是允许的。如果仔细研读评分标准，会发现即便是7分也是可以出错的，只要不影响交流就可以了。

本话题词汇储备：

Movie making

direction	导演	montage	剪辑
production	制片	recording, sound, recording	录音
adaptation	改编	dubbing	配音
scenario, screenplay, script	编剧	properties, props	道具

lighting	灯光	script	剧本
shooting	摄制	slow motion	慢镜头
special effects	特技	editing, cutting	剪接

Movie worker

cast	阵容	makeup girl	化妆师
director	导演	dialogue writer	对白作者
film star, movie star	电影明星	script writer	剧本作者
star, lead	主角	extra, walker-on	临时演员
support	配角	extra	特别客串
double, stand-in	替身演员	costume designer	服装设计员

Names to remember

导演：			
Steven Spielberg			史蒂文•斯皮尔伯格
Frank Darabont			弗兰克•达拉邦特
Ang Lee			李安
Zhang Yimou			张艺谋
演员：			
Angelina Jolie	安吉丽娜•朱莉	Maggie Cheung	张曼玉
Julia Roberts	朱莉亚•罗伯茨	Brad Pitt	布拉德•皮特
Sharon stone	莎朗•斯通	Nicolas Cage	尼古拉斯•凯奇
Monica Bellucci	莫妮卡•贝鲁奇	Tom Cruise	汤姆•克鲁斯
Jodie Foster	乔迪•福斯特	Tom Hanks	汤姆•汉克斯
Kristen Dunst	克里斯滕•邓斯特	Bruce Wills	布鲁斯•威利斯
Sandra Bullock	桑德拉•布洛克	Arnold Schwarzenegger	阿诺德•施瓦辛格
Zhang Ziyi	章子怡	Fat Chou	周润发
Michelle Yeoh	杨紫琼	Jet Lee	李连杰

Movies

Hero	英雄	The Promise	无极
Farewell My Concubine	霸王别姬	The Curse of Golden Flowers	满城尽带黄金甲
Baby Plan	宝贝计划	Crouching Tigers, Hidden Dragon	卧虎藏龙
The lord of the rings	指环王	Forrest Gump	阿甘正传
Brave Heart	勇敢的心	Roman Holiday	罗马假日
Waterloo Bridge	魂断蓝桥	Lion King	狮子王
Cinderella	灰姑娘	Avatar	阿凡达

有了上面的词汇储备，加上描述思路，描述一部电影就变得容易了。考试的时候，可以对着白纸上写的关键词进行描述。

本题的回答可以是：

Title: Well, I would like to describe a movie I have just watched last weekend. The title is Avatar.

Director: It is a 2009 American science fiction epic film written and directed by James-Cameron , who has been world-wide known since the Titanic.

Actors and actresses: I would say another reason that I chose to watch the movie is because it is acted by some of my favorite stars, such as Sam Worthington, Zoe Saldana, Sigourney Weaver, Michelle Rodriguez and Stephen Lang.

Plot: The film is set in the year 2154 on Pandora, a moon in the Alpha Centauri star system. Humans are engaged in mining Pandora's reserves of a precious mineral, called unobtanium, while the Na'vi—a race of indigenous humanoids—resist the colonists' expansion, which threatens the continued existence of the Na'vi and the Pandoran ecosystem. Therefore, a war between human and Na'vi happened.

Comment: Actually, I am not a movie goer, but I was fascinated by this movie, you know, I watched the 3D version, I would say, it gets the best video effect, it felt so real, as if I am in the movie, so I was so involved.

周计划提示

TIP 7：真实交际非常重要

为了准备考试，对部分答案进行背诵是值得提倡的，但是在考试的时候就要借用表演技能了，不能让考官感觉你在背诵。一旦考官发现考生对当前所谈论的 topic 有所准备，就会立刻转移话题。所以，预测考试将要出现的 topic 并进行准备虽然必要，但考生并不应该死记硬背某个固定的答案，尤其不能给考官造成“背诵答案”的印象。除了上面讲的要充分利用肢体语言、面部表情和目光接触外。也要注意适当的停顿和思考，给考官真实的感觉。将心里的答案无形地给考官表达出来。总之，无论内容是否真实，无论问题是否简单，都要和考官对话，讨论和交流。千万不要只顾自己说话，忘记和考官的真实交流。

TIP 8：保持镇静

在口语考试的时候经常会出现一些突发情况，尤其是在第三部分，经常会碰到所考话题太陌生或某个表达法不会。在面对这些问题的时候，一定要镇定自若。如果遇到自己不太熟悉或者根本一无所知的话题，考生应该说明自己对这一领域的陌生并尽可能的告诉考官自己所知道的一切，设法将话题转移到自己熟悉的领域，无论接下来的发言与话题是否相关，总比一言不发的效果好得多。在思索答案的时候，考生应该学会采取一些拖延时间的策略。毕竟考核的核心是语言而不是内容。如考官问你：“What flowers get special meaning in China?”不懂花，不能成为你雅思考低分的原因。但要巧妙处理问题，转移困难的核心。

考生大可以坦然告诉考官对花语了解甚少，但对某一种花有所了解，然后将自己知道的部分用恰当的语言表达出来就可以了。考官看的是你如何表达自己知道的内容，不会因为你不懂花而为难你。况且，生僻的话题绝对是少数。

除了话题陌生外，还有一种情况就是突然想不起某个词或者根本不知道某个表达法该怎么说。这个时候，一定要结合非语言的手段，用迂回的方式表达出要表达的意思。不要告诉考官你不知道，将这个语言的不足隐藏好就可以了。 如考 instrument 的时候有人想说自己会弹古筝。可是不知道该怎么表达这种乐器，只好放弃。其实大可不必。你完全可以说：“I quite like guzheng, which is 21 string traditional Chinese instrument.”考官一听就明白了。虽然他不一定知道古筝，但他知道是 21 弦的乐器。考官会为你的生词处理技巧加分的。

Part 3

1. Do you have any favourite film stars (or actors or actresses)? （*provide information*）

—Yes, my favourite movie star is Jackie Chen, who is a Kungfu movie star, I like him because he combined serious Chinese Kungfu with humor, and played a significant role in improving Chinese Kungfu and movie making. I like him also because he is a great person in real life, he did a lot of work for charity. So in my mind, he is a real hero, like the ones he acted in his movies.

2. Do you and your parents like to watch the same kinds of films? （*comparing*）

—Well, not really, although I hope so. My parents and I are two generations, grown up in very different environment. My generation is called “Digital Generation”, so I like the movies with the best audio and video effect, while my parents enjoy something more emotional and patriotic, or I may say, they focus more on the plot.

3. What sorts of films do you think are unsuitable for children to watch? （*provide information*）

—Generally speaking, it is hard to have a clear cut for what is suitable for children and what is not. But the movies with too much violence and porn are definitely unsuitable, because children tend to believe what they see and hear real, they might be misled easily.

4. Is there any difference between the kinds of films people in China watch today and the kinds of films they watched before (for example, 20～50 years ago)? （*comparing*）

—Well, I guess there are many differences, such as themes, variety and technique used for movie making. 50 years ago, the themes of movies were only patriotic, but today, there are more themes, and also many technologies have been used in movie making nowadays.

5. In general, do you think films (popular movies) have any educational value? (*give opinions and reasons*)

—Sure, for example, there are a lot of movies about global warming, which shock and scare the audience, and eventually raise people’s awareness of environment protection. And for another example, many action movies show us the result of committing crimes, which also warn the public do not take risks.

6. Do you prefer to watch foreign films or domestically made (Chinese) films? (*contrast*)

—Well, I think both have their advantages, but if I have to choose one, I would say I prefer foreign films, especially Hollywood movies, because they provide very good video effect, which is very entertaining and eye-catching.

7. What are the most common themes of films today? (*providing information*)

—Well, it is hard to say, because the movie industry has developed greatly in the last several years, there are various kinds of themes, but, comparatively speaking, global warming, environment protection, space exploring ect. are very widely concerned. I think to a certain extent, movies are commercial products, so it has to try to meet the need of market or public interest, so movies would normally reflect the contemporary problems people face.

8. Have you ever been confused by the difference between the "academic" English you learned in school and the English used in films? (*Explaining*)

—Yes, very often actually, because the English I learned in school is standard English with few slang and colloquial expressions. Once I used some phrases I have picked up in the movies in my thesis writing, as a result I got very low score in the language aspect.

9. Do you think watching foreign movies in English can help you (or help people) learn English? (*Giving opinions and reasons*)

—Sure, especially for my speaking and listening, the language used in movies are very idiomatic and can be used in daily life, so it is a very good learning resource for the learners who have no opportunity to be exposed to English speaking environment.

10. Can you suggest some ways that the film industry could use to attract a larger audience to their films? (*Suggesting*)

—Well, there should be many ways that can be used to attract audience. For example, asking the most popular movie stars to act the movie, because many fans will go to watch the movie just because of the stars without thinking of the actual content of the movie. What is more, using modern technology to perfect the audio and video effect is a good way, because nowadays people are very concerned about these of a movie.

周计划提示

TIP 9: 注意答案的个性

雅思考试在中国已经有多年了，由于各种版本机经的贡献，绝大多数口语考题考生在考前都有所了解，并作了相应的准备。但非常遗憾的是，各个考生都互相借鉴甚至抄袭，最后导致答案千篇一律、过度雷同，使答案太俗套，不具备个性。其结果是，考生自我感觉良好，但分数差强人意，甚至是大出意料。其实，原因很简单。雅思考核的是考生对语言的实际运用能力。每个考生的情况不一样，所以在被问到同样一个问题的时候，答案应该是不一样的。如果完全一样，那么答案就是死记硬背的。这并不是口语能力的体现而是背诵能力的体现。

如："How are you?" 经常是考官见到考生后常问的问题。很多中国考生习惯性地回答道："Fine, thank you, and you?" 却不知道这是考官最不喜欢的答案，这个答案在国外几乎已经成了识别一个中国人的标志了。其实，即便是对这样一个简单的问题，我们也有很多种答法，如：I am ok; Pretty good ; Can't be better ; I am doing well; I am ok; Just a little nervous 等。考生可以给出很多更具体、更代表当时情况和自己个性的答案。这样会让考官耳目一新，自然会对考生产生不错的印象。

TIP 10：建立良好第一印象

虽然考试是从考官打开录音设备开始，但是，只要进了考场，考生所说的每一句话都会影响到考官对考生的第一印象。而这一印象经常是考官给考生定级定分的一个非常重要的参考依据。而且经常会影响到考官在考试过程中对问题的选择。例如：如果考官对某位考生的第一印象是该考生英语水平非常有限，那么后面的问题也就会非常简单，这样就从根本上剥夺了考生拿高分的可能性。所以，考生在进考场后回答的每一个问题，都要符合口语评分标准，即从语音语调、词汇语法和流畅连贯各个方面做到恰到好处。

TIP 11：注意句型

句型或者语法是四个评分标准中的一个重要标准。所以，在整个考试的过程中，考生要有意识地变换自己的句型，不要反复使用同样一个句型。不管某个句型多么好，如果反复使用，同样会反映出考生句型结构多样性不足。更不用说很多考生只会用主谓宾、主系表结构。如：当考官问道："Where do you come from?" 的时候。很多考生的答案是："I am from China." 或 "I am from Beijing, the capital of China." 等，这都体现句型结构不够丰富。大家要想着如何体现自己语言的潜力和功底，同时又保证语言自然流畅，不至于太过书面化。如：

- Well, I was born in the city of Yi Chang, which is famous for the Three Gorges.
- I am a local man, and I live in Haidian district, my home is very close to the Friendship Hotel, which is one of the most famous hotels in Beijing.

总之，考生要根据自己的实际情况去构思，去想该如何表达自己的这些信息，并反复操练，达到熟练程度，以至考试的时候能不假思索地给出答案。

TIP 12：不要紧张但要有紧迫感

在考试过程中感到紧张是正常的现象。考官也很清楚这一点，所以没有必要告诉考官 "I am very nervous."。在考试开始以前，考生应该尽量缓解自己的紧张情绪。例如：在等候考试开始的时候，做几个深呼吸；回忆生活中的趣事；以自我肯定的方式安慰自己等。在考试的过程中，回答难度较大的问题之前，考生可以利用片刻时间做个深呼吸，稳定自己的情绪，以求表现得更好。很多考生准备得十分充分，但由于过度紧张导致大脑一片空白，对任何话题都不能正常发挥。在学习过程中培养自信也非常重要，自信的人往往不会紧张。

但也有考生显得太过松散。不紧张是好事，有助于超常发挥，但是如果太松散，就缺少紧迫感，会导致不够流畅、节奏太慢。单位时间内给出的语言样本太少，也会影响得分。

TIP 13：声音控制很重要

在雅思口语考试中，考生应该注意控制自己的声音大小。既要确保考官能够听清楚，也要避免声音过大使其烦躁。还要注意，声音应该具有一定的力度，否则会显得缺乏信心。

此外，人们在紧张的时候，语速通常会加快，在考试过程中，尤其是当考生的发音不够标准时，这可能会妨碍考官听清答案。

总之，考生要想尽一切办法给考官留下良好的印象。尤其是在英语的语音语调，句型结构，流畅连贯和交际各个方面都要让他觉得你的语言足以到英美国家生存、学习、甚至工作。所以在学习英语的同时大家也要充分了解西方国家的文化和风俗习惯，让考官感觉他在和一个懂得英语国家文化的人聊天。达到一种最自然的状态，考试的分数必然低不了。最后提醒各位考生，必须提前了解考试流程，确保考试万无一失。由于口语考试的程式具有统一的标准，考官必须按照标准程序提问并引导考试进程，以确保考试的公平。所以，请务必不要：向考官询问私人问题；在考试结束时询问自己的得分；要求考官对自己的表现发表评论或给予反馈意见。要从进考场到离开，都给考官留下一个好印象。

星期四
雅思口语思路 3、5、7

礼物是雅思口语考试非常高频的话题，因为礼物是所有人都难以避免的。而且，每个国家和地方因文化不同对于礼物的理解又有差别。能用英语表达文化差异是雅思口语考试的重要考点。所以，跟礼物相关的问题反复在口语第 1、2、3 部分出现。因此，对这个话题进行充足的准备非常重要。今天，我们详尽地学习 gift 这个话题，并以此为主线，学习雅思口语考试第 1、2、3 部分的答题思路。概括起来，第 1 部分的问题有 3 个常用的答题思路；第 2 部分有 5 种最常用的描写思路；第 3 部分主要有 7 种考点。下面，我们通过“礼物”逐一学习。

一、与 Gift 有关的问题

Part 1

1. Do you often give gifts to other people?
2. On what occasions do you give gifts?
3. What kinds of things do people in China give each other as gifts?
4. Do you think gift-giving is very important?
5. Do you think the price of the gift matters?

Part 2

Describe a special gift that you (recently) gave to a friend.

You should say:

what the gift was

when you gave this gift

who you gave it to

and explain why you chose that particular gift.

Possible follow-up questions:

1. Was he/she very grateful?
2. Would you like to receive this same gift from someone?

Part 3

1. Why is gift-giving important? (*explain*)
2. In China, what sort of things can not be given as gifts? (*give information*)
3. What kind of gift do you think people will give in future?(*Speculate*)
4. Do you think it's suitable to give money as a gift? (*give opinion and reasons*)
5. How to make sure the receiver likes the gift you send? (*suggest*)
6. What is the difference between gift and bribe? (*compare & contrast*)
7. Why do you think gift sending may lead to misunderstanding? (*Justify or defend your opinion*)

二、Part 1 的 3 个发展答题思路

如前所述，第 1 部分问题的答案不可以太简单。要尽可能地体现自己语言的流畅和连贯。为了保证对任何问题，都能用两三句话来作答，必须有拓展答案的意识和相应的方法。有三种思路，可以保证这一部分的答案够长，对任何问题，永远有话可说。这些思路是：

1. 三步走：铺垫+答案+解释
2. 一般到具体（general to specific）
3. 例证（exemplification）

下面我们在具体例子中体验学习这些思路。

1. Do you often give gifts to other people?

周计划提示

常用答题思路之一：三步走：铺垫+答案+解释

很多问题，让考生觉得无从下手，可能是问题过于简单，如：yes/no 的问题，也可能是缺少思考时间，还有可能是对相关知识了解不够，所以经常会给出过于简单或宽泛的答案，其句型和词汇的使用，自然不理想，严重影响得分。对于这种问题，非常常用的一个答题思路是：三步走 （铺垫+答案+解释），也就是说先提供一点背景知识作为铺垫，然后在此基础上给出答案，最后给出一定的解释，这样就可以保证无论问题多么简单，答案都一定会有三句以上，从而体现出考生的语言“惯性”和流畅性。

如：Do you often do things with others in a group (or with your friends)?

—Well, you know I am a very introvert person, **so I seldom do things with others in a group, I much prefer to do things by myself**, because I often feel nervous even uncomfortable to be with others.

其中，so I seldom do things with others in a group, I much prefer to do things by myself 是答案，而它前面的一句就是背景铺垫，后面的一句则是进一步解释或者发展。这样一来，问题虽然简单，但答案还是能充分体现考生口语水平的。

本题参考答案：

—Well, you know, I am a salesman, so interpersonal relationship is very important for me. Therefore, giving gifts is not only a part of my life, but also a part of my work. By exchanging gifts, I showed my willingness to be friends with others, so I made many friends.

2. On what occasions do you give gifts?

周计划提示

常用答题思路之二：一般到具体（general to specific）

一般到具体（general to specific）是个非常常用的答题思路，也就是先从整体上回答，然后具体解释，以保证答案的全面。同时，这种思路也给考生留出充足的时间构思具体该怎么往下说，

如：What kinds of leisure time activities are popular with young people today?

—Well, it is hard to say, because there are many activities that are popular among young people, but students often play computer games when they are free, while those who get jobs often go to KTV to release the tension they get from their work.

其中，there are many activities that are popular among young people 就是一般的回答，这个句子放在任何地方都准确，在任何人身上都说得通，而且，说出这一句几乎不用思考，所以在说的同时可以思考下面具体的该怎么回答。后面分别举了两个例子，一个是在校学生，一个是已经工作的年轻人。这样回答既完整有序，又有说服力，是一个可以多次使用的回答思路。

本题参考答案：

—Well, I send gifts on many occasions. For example, I send people gifts on festivals, such as on Valentine's Day I send gifts to my girl friend, and I also send people gifts on special days, including wedding ceremonies and opening ceremonies. What's more, I sometimes send gifts to show my gratefulness to those who helped me.

3. What kinds of things do people in China give each other as gifts? 一般到具体

本题参考答案：

—Well, I think it depends on the situation, but generally speaking, everything can be a gift if you get a good reason. For example, cash or red package is a very common gift, and cigarettes and alcohol is often sent when visiting relatives or friends.

4. Do you think gift-giving is very important? 举例说明

周计划提示

常用答题思路之三：例证（exemplification）

当一个问题太大、太泛、无从下手的时候，就采用例证法。举例说明是非常有效的论证方法。而且，举例将单纯的辩论转换成讲述故事，这样在语言使用上也要容易地多。

本题参考答案：

—Sure, because it is a way for us to show our love, care or gratefulness. For example, on festivals I send gifts to my friends and relatives, and they gave me gifts as well, so we were very happy, because we know that we care each other, and we are remembered and we are important. I may say, to a certain extent, it helps to make a more harmonious society.

5．Do you think the price of the gift matters?

本题参考答案：

—Surely not, what really matters is the meaning or the reason why gift is given, but of course the price is often a reference for people to choose a gift.

三、Part 2 的 5 个描写思路

Describe a special gift that you (recently) gave to a friend. You should say: what the gift was when you gave this gift who you gave it to and explain why you chose that particular gift.

Possible follow-up questions:

1．Was he/she very grateful?

2．Would you like to receive this same gift from someone?

本题分析：

描写一个礼物，其本质是要考生描写一个物体。对物体进行描写，很多考生没有思路或想法，通常不知道从哪里下手，因此常常在表达出礼物是什么、谁送的之后，就没话可说了。然而，第 2 部分的答案要求有两分钟的长度，因此，答题思路非常重要。描写物体可以从回答下面 5 个问题着手：

1．这个礼物是什么？

2．这个礼物是送给谁的？

3．你为什么要送给他/她这个礼物？

4．这个礼物有什么用途或功能？

5．这个礼物对你和接受礼物的人有什么影响？

按这个思路回答就可以说：

1．我要描写的礼物是一个 MP4。

2．这个礼物是送给我最要好的朋友 Tomy 的。

3．我送他这个礼物是因为他要出国学习了，我十分不舍。

4．用这个礼物，他可以听音乐，看电影，玩游戏等，可以帮他渡过在国外的孤独时光。

5．这个礼物是我们友谊的象征，我想让他明白，无论他走到哪里，我都是他最好的朋

友，当他有困难的时候，我永远都会给他帮助。我想我们的友谊会长存，并且越来越深厚。

这样这个话题就有足够的内容可以说了，相信口语考试的时候一定会有不错的分数。

本题参考答案：

I would like to describe a gift that I have recently given to my best friend Tomy, it is an MP4 produced by Aigo Company. You know, Tomy and I have been best friend for years, but now he is going to America for further education, I am very upset, but I have to congratulate him, because this will be very good for his life.

I chose the gift for him because it gets many functions. With the MP4, he can listen to music, play games, and watch movies, so I think it would help him to kill time when he is alone in America.

I gave the gift to him because I wanted him to know that wherever he went, he was not alone. I would always be ready for help. I think he got the message. I think we will be friends forever.

以此为例，实物描写的思路可提炼为：

- 物体是什么？（可以对外形稍加描写）
- 物体的功能或作用是什么？
- 该物体和什么人相关？（对物体描写结合人物或渗透情感，会让描写上一个台阶）
- 物体对所涉及人的影响

周计划提示

Part 2 最常考的话题有五种类型：

1. 实物描写
2. 人物、动物描写
3. 事件、活动描写
4. 地点、场所描写
5. 故事、经历描写

Part 2 的5个宏观描写思路归纳如下：

1. 实物描写（见上）
2. 人物、动物描写

	人物	动物
外貌	典型人物外貌特征	动物天然外貌特征，人为装饰
性格特征	人物性格特征说明	动物性格特点
举例说明	用一小事证明其性格特征	小故事说明其性格特征
总体评价	该人对本人的影响	该动物的影响

3. 事件、活动描写
   - 什么活动？

- 活动的规则是什么？
- 这个活动的意义是什么？
- 我的个人感受是什么？

4. 地点、场所描写
   - 入场顺序
   - 由近及远

5. 故事、经历描写
   - When（什么时候）
   - Where（什么地点）
   - Who（涉及什么人）
   - What（发生什么事）
   - Why（为什么发生）
   - How（如何结尾）

四、Part 3 的 7 个考点

Part 3

1. Why is gift-giving important? (*explain*)
2. In China, What sort of things can not be given as gifts? (*give information*)
3. What kind of gift do you think people will give in future?(*speculate*)
4. Do you think it's suitable to give money as a gift? (*give opinion and reasons*)
5. How to make sure the receiver likes the gift you send? (*suggest*)
6. What is the difference between gift and bribe? (compare & contrast)
7. Why do you think gift sending may lead to misunderstanding? (Justifying or defending your opinion)

第 3 部分涉及 7 个主要考点：

1. Explaining	explaining how or why certain situations exist
2. Giving information	give several examples of something, add some extra information or personal comments.
3. Speculating	guessing about the past, the present and the future
4. Giving your opinions and reasons	answering questions that begin with words such as, "How well …?", "How effective …?","How much …?","How important …?","Do you think …?"or "Should …?"
5. Suggesting	suggesting possible ways to solve a problem; and suggesting advice for people.
6. Comparing and contrasting	Comparing the differences between older and younger people; differences between males and females; differences between a situation today and the situation in previous years; differences between rural and urban areas.
7. Justifying or defending your opinion	Sometimes the examiner will challenge your opinion to see if you can give some evidence or good reasons for your opinion.

Other part 3 questions related to gifts

1. What are some of the gift-giving customs in China?
2. Besides special occasions such as birthdays and festivals, what are some other reasons why people give presents to others?
3. Do you think people in China should give presents on western festivals such as Christmas?
4. Is it difficult to choose presents for people?
5. Do advertisements influence people's choices when they are buying gifts?
6. Compare the differences between gifts for children and gifts for adults.
7. Do you think that expensive gifts are a sign of true friendship?
8. What is the difference between a "precious" gift and a "valuable" gift?
9. What would be a suitable gift when saying goodbye to someone after a visit?
10. What are some of the possible different reasons why give gifts to other people?

星期五

雅思口语 Part 1 考点汇总

雅思口语第一部分的考试主要考核日常生活的话题，不会涉及政治、宗教和专业话题。其考试的话题是任何一个考生都能有话可说，以此达到公平的目的。但第1部分考试的话题也非常广，涉及个人信息、工作学习、饮食起居、休闲娱乐、兴趣爱好、科技媒体、节假庆典、动物环境、体育健身、人际交往、交通旅行、气候天气等日常生活的方方面面。其目的是看考生是否能用英语谈论所有日常话题，也就是从广度上考核考生。

一、Part 1 最常见考试话题

个人信息	
Names; Your Home (Your Accommodation); Family; Age; Plans & Goals(ambitions)	考生要对个人的信息作充足的准备。尤其是关于自己的姓名、家庭、家乡、个人目标等，要做到随问随答。因此准备好个人信息的同时，也要储备好相关词汇和表达法，这些信息往往会在考试热身的时候考到，也就是会在考生没有完全进入考试状态的时候考，因此，需要考生通过精心准备，达到一定的熟练程度，才能在考试的时候对答如流，给考官留下良好的第一印象。
工作学习	
Your Studies; Your Primary School; Your Secondary School; your Work	考官会根据考生的实际情况来询问考生的工作或学习。对于在校学生，考官更多会问到考生的学习及对未来工作的打算；而对已经工作的人员则是询问其工作情况，比如以前、现在做什么工作，以及将来想做什么样的工作，有时候也会询问其以前的学习情况。总之，对学习和工作，考生也要能有比较详细而充分的准备。不要出现考官问到你在哪里学习，还不知道自己学校的名字怎么表达这样的情况。
饮食起居	
Daily Routine; Time; Food/Cooking;	一日三餐是每个人都难以回避的话题。每个人有不同的饮食习惯、有不同的口味喜好。有人喜欢蔬菜水果，也有人喜欢鸡鸭鱼肉；有人喜欢自己烹饪，也有人喜欢下馆子。这些都是考生需要准备，并能熟练表

Meals; Fruits and Vegetables; Restaurants; Housework; Private Gardens	达的内容。另外，考生的日常生活习惯，起居作息时间，家务等，都是生存英语的一部分，也需要考生能流畅表达。
休闲娱乐	
Leisure Time & Relaxing; Evenings; Weekends; Shopping; Films; Music; Games; Reading; Art; Art Galleries and Museums; Clothes and Fashion; Outdoor Activities; Going Out; Parks and Public Gardens	几乎每一次口语考试都有关于娱乐的话题。业余生活是西方人非常重视的，他们在日常生活中会花费很多精力和时间来想尽办法消遣。谈论业余活动也是朋友见面必不可少的话题。正因如此，休闲娱乐就成了雅思口语考试的必考话题。但每一考的话题都不一样，早些时候直接询问业余干什么，近期的考试往往具体到各个话题，比如音乐、电视、电影、购物、游戏、阅读、艺术、博物馆、服装、户外运动、公园等，只要是业余能玩的，就都会考到。学英语，就要先从学玩开始。
兴趣爱好	
Collecting; Colours; Dance; Drawing or Painting; Photography; Writing	“Do you like dancing/ drawing/ photographing/ writing/ collecting?” 很多话题，考官都从考生的喜好开始问起，然后逐渐提高难度。但轻松表达个人喜好是最为基础的口语考试内容。
科技媒体	
Newspapers; News; Magazines and Newspapers; Advertisements; Mobile Phones; Telephones; Television and Radio;	电脑、网络、电视、广播、电话、报纸、杂志等广泛应用于人民日常生活的科技媒体是雅思口语考试必须准备的话题。

The Internet; Computers	
节假庆典	
Birthdays; Holidays ; Parties; festivals	能用英语谈论各种节日文化、假期活动、以及各种庆典聚会，是非常重要的口语能力。
动物环境	
Animals; Birds; pets; Sounds (Noises)	西方人有很强的动物、环境保护意识。他们热爱动物、喜欢养宠物、主张动物权；热爱大自然，倡导保护环境。对动物和环境的关注不仅体现在他们的日常生活中，更体现在雅思口语考题中。
体育健身	
Sport/Exercise; Sports Teams; Swimming; cycling	西方人喜欢利用自己的业余时间强身健体，他们去健身房，到郊外、骑车、游泳，只要能锻炼身体，能享受大自然，能长肌肉，他们都热衷。自然的，他们也就喜欢谈论这个话题。而中国人在业余时间都喜欢学习，学电脑，学外语，所以当谈到或考到相关话题，经常有些不知所措。
人际交往	
Friends; Neighbours; Visitors; Teachers; Gifts; Flowers; Letters & Emails; Languages	结交朋友，走亲访友，书信来往，赠礼送花等话题经常因国家或文化不同而不同，因此谈论这些文化以及各国文化的不同，也是雅思口语经常考到的话题。
交通旅行	
Transportation; Bicycles; Driving a Car; Travelling	随着经济的发展，交通工具越来越多样化，但交通问题也随之多了起来。谈论交通就成了一个日常话题。到英美国家学习和工作的人，也必须具备相关的语言能力。所以，雅思口语必考。

气候天气	
Seasons; Climate; Weather; Rain	英国人喜欢谈论天气。英国天气尤其是冬天的天气是十分糟糕的。因为，几乎见不着阳光，总是阴沉着，经常下雨。而且夏天容易出现一天四季的现象，所以，让英国人非常苦恼。也正因为如此，久居其中的人们才形成了谈论天气的习惯。另外，通过谈论天气来寒暄也就自然回避了“您吃了吗？”之类的尴尬和“您去哪儿？”的隐私话题。去英国前，一定要先学会谈论天气。

二、Part 1 常见疑问

很多考生对第1部分的考试有很多疑问，下面我们来逐一解决。

1．听不懂考官问题的时候怎么办？

偶尔有听不懂的问题没有关系，可以让考官重复。当然，不能总是：“I beg your pardon?”最好能换不同的方式来问，比如：“Do you mean …? ”、“I am not sure, but do you mean I should tell you …?” 等。要知道：“Asking for clarification is a good communication skill and the examiner takes into consideration your communication skills when giving you your score.”

2．考官让我重复我的话意味着什么？

考官让你重复答案，意味着combination of two things — imperfect pronunciation and an unsuitable choice of words。也就是说，如果你发音清晰准确，但措辞不清楚，考官一般不会让你重复；如果你措辞准确，但发音不够完美，考官也不会让你重复。所以当考官让你重复的时候，最好换一个表达法把刚说的一个答案复述一遍。也可以考虑加一个例子来说明。或者用“In other words, …” or “What I mean is, …”等表达法来解释或补充说明。

3．考官打断我意味着什么？

如果考官打断你，不要担心，更不要烦躁。考官有责任控制考试时间以确保考试顺利进行。考试的三个部分有严格的考试时间限制，所以，考官必须在必要的时候打断你。

4．口语答案的内容必须都真实吗？

雅思口语考试是纯语言测试，不考核内容。得分以你使用的语言质量来给分。内容的多少和好坏对分数有一定影响。但是，真实度不会影响得分。有时候为了体现自己的语言水平，比如词汇量，可以适当说一些不真实的信息。考官关注的也是你的口语能力，而不是你说话的内容。当然，一切照实回答可以减少思考的时间，也会增加考试进程的流畅感。

5．考试的时候我能用我背诵好的答案吗？

雅思备考是必须的。但更多地应该提高自己的语言应用水平。对常用的词汇、词组和句型也可以适当记忆，并多次使用，内化为自己的能力。如果是准备好的答案，回答的时候面部表情和肢体语言都会让考官发现你是在背诵答案，考官因此会换题或扣分。因为，雅思考试的目的是考核考生的英语应用能力，而不是背诵能力。如果真要用背诵的答案，也需要练习最基本的“表演”技能，背台词的时候，不能让观众听出来你在背诵。最好不要完全背诵答案，而是记忆一个答题思路或结构。每次回答类似问题的时候都做适当修改，这样就可以回避背诵嫌疑。

6．第1部分的词汇使用应该把握一个什么样的度？

在第一部分的考试中，考生同样要体现自己的词汇量。但是，第一部分题目的特点决定了不能使用太学术的词汇。尤其要注意很多雅思词汇书收集的词汇都是雅思阅读或写作词汇，而不是口语词汇，所以使用那些雅思书上的词汇不一定能给你带来好的雅思口语成绩。雅思口语第一部分最好的答案是自然、流畅的语言，也就是最常用的语言。

总之，要想在第一部分拿到一个不错的分数，应该让考官感觉你有意愿、有能力和考官针对所有话题进行问答，充分体现你的词汇量、语法准确性和句型多样性，同时注意答案的个性。让考官感觉他在和一个考生用英语聊天，其过程是愉快的，不做作，这样的考试分数一定是最高的。

星期六 雅思口语 Part 2 话题总结

虽然第二部分的考题非常多，但是仔细分析每次考试的考题不难发现，雅思口语话题不管怎么换，都是换汤不换药。也就是说，考点并没有换。第 2 部分无非就是让考生描写一个人物、动物、地点、事物、活动、事件、故事或经历。下面的表格就总结了第 2 部分几乎所有考过的话题。

一、Part 2 常见考试话题总结

人物

1. Your Best Friend	2. A Childhood Friend
3. A Family Friend	4. A Friend
5. A Leader	6. The Oldest Person You Know
7. An Old Person	8. An Old Person Who You Admire
9. An Interesting Old Person	10. A Child You Know
11. A Teenager You Know	12. Someone You Like to Spend Time With
13. Two People from the Same Family	14. A Famous Person
15. A School Friend	16. An Intelligent Person
17. A Character From a Childhood Story	18. A Good Neighbour
19. An Adventurous Person	20. A Person Who Has Visited Your Home
21. A Person Who Is Good at His/Her Job	22. Someone Who Is Good at Cooking
23. A Person Who Likes to Help Others	24. A Person Who Took Care of You in Your Childhood
25. A Person You Enjoy Talking With	26. A Person You Live With
27. A Family Member	28. A Person You Visited
29. A Person You Would Like to Be Similar to	30. Someone Who Does Something Well
31. Someone Who Gave You Important Help	32. A Competition Winner
33. Someone Who Spoke a Different Language	34. Someone You Enjoy Spending Time with

动物

1. A Domesticated Animal	2. A Wild Animal from Your Country
3. A Wild Animal	4. An Interesting Animal

地点

1. A Building in Your Hometown
2. A Building in Your School or University
3. A Cafe or Restaurant
4. A Garden
5. A Hotel
6. A Leisure Centre
7. A Library
8. A Modern Building
9. A Place Where People Listen to Music
10. A Place for Swimming
11. A Place for Shopping
12. A Place with a Lot of Water
13. A Polluted City
14. A Polluted Place
15. An Ideal Park
16. An Historic Site
17. Your Childhood Home
18. Your Childhood Room
19. Your Favourite Part of Your Hometown
20. A Restaurant You Like
21. A Small Shop
22. A Tourist Attraction
23. An Open-air Market
24. Ideal Home
25. A City You Have Visited or Lived in
26. Your Work or Study Place
27. A (Place In A) City You Visited

实物

1. Something You Made by Hand
2. A Magazine
3. An Old Thing in Your Family
4. Clothing for Special Occasions
5. A Childhood Present
6. A Family Photo
7. A Photograph That You Like
8. A Car or Vehicle You Would Like to Have
9. Favourite Means Of Transportation
10. A Childhood Toy
11. A Gift
12. A Gift You Gave
13. A Piece Of Equipment
14. A Piece Of Furniture
15. A Work Of Art
16. An Electrical/Electronic Product
17. Something You Want to Buy
18. Something You Lost

抽象事物

1. An Interesting Subject
2. An Organization
3. Another Language
4. Art or Music
5. Something that Helped You Learn a Language
6. Something You Saved For
7. Something You Would Like to Learn
8. A Piece of Good News by Phone
9. A Project or Homework Assignment
10. An Important Letter You Wrote
11. A Letter or Card You Received
12. An Email or Postcard
13. A Sport You Played in Childhood
14. A Newspaper or Magazine Article
15. A Newspaper You Like to Read
16. Favourite Weather
17. The Perfect Climate
18. Your Favourite Season
19. A Small Business You Would Like To Own
20. An Advertisement
21. A Childhood Game
22. A Childhood Song or Melody
23. A Class Or Course
24. A Foreign Culture

25. A Job
26. A Job You Did Quickly
27. A Language Skill
28. A Performance
29. A Practical Skill
30. A Radio Program
31. A Skill You Recently Learned
32. Your Favourite Subject at School
33. A Course You Would Like to Take
34. A TV or Radio Program
35. A Type of Film
36. A Way to Relax
37. A Website
38. An Exciting Sport
39. An Exhibition
40. Future Work Plans
41. A Good Law

活动

1. A Childhood Activity
2. A Group Activity
3. A Leisure Activity
4. A New or Exciting Activity
5. A Physical Activity
6. An Artistic Activity
7. An Outdoor Activity
8. An English Class Activity

事件

1. A Family Event
2. A Sports Event
3. A Public Event
4. A Recent Happy Event
5. A Happy Event
6. A Traditional Event in Your Country
7. A Local Event

故事

1. A Book
2. A Book You Enjoyed as a Child
3. A Book You Enjoyed Reading
4. A Book You Recently Read
5. A Book You Would Like to Read Again
6. The Latest Book You Have Read
7. Some Interesting News
8. Some Recent News
9. A Story from TV
10. An (Interesting) Film
11. A Well-known Story from Your Country

经历

1. Travel to Somewhere in the World
2. A Busy Time
3. Last Weekend
4. An Unhappy Shopping Experience
5. An Interesting Talk (Speech)
6. An Occasion When You Were Late
7. An Important Decision
8. School Holidays
9. Some Advice You Received
10. Studying IELTS
11. Leisure Time
12. Living in a Place in Another Country
13. A Science Lesson
14. A Traffic Jam
15. A Time When You Helped Someone
16. An Interesting Or Unusual Thing You Did Recently
17. A Walk
18. A Conversation You Had

19. A Happy Childhood Memory	20. A Journey with Your Friends
21. A Lesson Class or Training Session	22. A Long Journey
23. A Meal For Your Friends	24. A Party
25. A Picnic or Outdoor Meal	26. A Positive Change
27. A Recent Change	28. A Special Meal
29. A Stage in Your Life you Enjoyed	30. A Stage of Your Life
31. A Success You Have Had	32. A Trip
33. An Educational Trip	34. Success
35. A Future Change	36. A Healthy Habit

二、Part 2 常见疑问

1．第2部分主要考核什么技能？

第2部分是考生英语综合运用能力的体现。口语考试的4个评分标准——语音、语法、词汇、流畅和连贯都会涉及，但是流畅和连贯是最容易在这一部分受到关注的。

2．有人说第2部分的答案就像是小型演讲，是这样吗？

不。应该像是在用自然的语气讲述一个小故事。最好不要逐词逐句地背诵一个答案，如果考官发现你的答案是背诵的，你的最终得分会受到影响。

3．第2部分审题需要注意什么？

在审第2部分题目的时候，要特别留意卡片上第1句话的关键形容词或副词。如 describe an interesting news 中的 interesting 是最重要的修饰词。一定要在答案中体现。如果你随便描写了一则新闻，但没有任何趣味性，这对分数肯定是有很大影响的。

另外，you should say 后面的内容一定要涵盖，否则有答非所问的嫌疑。当然，考生可以补充其他与考题相关的内容。

4．如何最有效地使用这一分钟的准备时间？

这一分钟的准备时间主要是给考生思考说什么、怎么说。考生需要集中注意力，回忆复习阶段有没有准备好的类似的答案。当确定好说什么之后，一定要特别留意时态，并开始集思广益。可以用铅笔在白纸上写出关键词，以便在回答的时候可以参考这些关键词。但要特别提醒的是：不要写完整的句子，准备时间非常有限、也非常宝贵，没有时间把什么都写下来。思考的时间主要要用在宏观思路上，至于细节，可以在说的时候，一边说一边思考。

5．该如何开始第2部分的答题？

第2部分虽然比较长，但并不要求特别正式。所以，可以以"I would like to describe a ... who / which..."来开头，直奔主题。开头用一个关系从句非常好，一是容易准备，另外，一开始就给考官一个从句，让考官知道考生可以准确使用复杂句。这是5分和6分答案的最本质区别。

6．第2部分主要考哪些语法点？

第2部分考核考生的综合语言能力，所有语法点都有可能涉及，这取决于具体考题和考生的答题思路。但是有 6 个语法现象是考生需要重点掌握的。它们是：动词时态；从句；人称代词 **he, him, his, she** 和 **her** 的准确性和一致性；间接引语；情态动词和条件从句。

7．如果考官给我的考题，我没有什么话可说，能要求换个话题吗？

要特别提醒考生的是，第 2 部分考官是不会换题的，即便考生要求换，考官也不会换。如果考生提出换题，等于自己承认不能回答这个问题，而雅思口语的最终考点是看考生是否能用英语对任何日常话题进行讨论，所以，建议考生不要自己告诉考官你不会。

其实，即便你说的话题完全是你自己的亲身体验，考官也未必知道或者说相信，也就是说，万一碰到一个自己没有相关体验的话题，就编一个。没有亲身经历过，一定听过看过，哪怕是类似的也可以。只不过在回答的时候不要让考官觉察到这是编的。

8．如何结束第 2 部分的考试？

很多考生说完了自己的答案就停下来等考官的指示，这是不对的。如果考官没有打断你，就意味着你还有时间可以继续说。如果你不暗示考官你已经说完，就容易冷场，这种瞬间的安静会让考官对你的整体印象分大打折扣。所以，当你答到一分半钟以上的时候，你可以随时根据需要停下来，但先要对考官说"That's all, thank you."提示考官进入下一个环节。如果考试时间还不到一分半钟，建议考生不要自己停下来，否则会因语言样本不够，影响考官打分。如果你的确没有新的内容增加，可以考虑把已经说过的答案总结一下。

9．第 2 部分描写完后，考官追问的两个小问题该如何回答？

首先，不是每个考生都会被追问，考官追问主要是想弄清楚考生在描述过程中提出的某些问题。一般追问的问题都是 yes/no 问题。考生只要简要回答就可以。但要注意，不能只是说一个 yes 或者 no。

星期日

雅思口语 Part 3 考点分析

第 3 部分考官有两个目的，一个是考察考生使用高分词汇、语法的能力和英语表达的连贯性；另一个是考核考生的语言上限。

第 3 部分的词汇使用应该比第 1、2 部分的要正式、复杂，但又不至于像写作词汇那样，否则就有点文绉绉的感觉了。简而言之，就是一个受过良好教育的人应该能够使用的词汇。

第 3 部分经常讨论的是比较复杂的问题，也就是给考生机会体现自己语言连贯的机会。讨论复杂问题所用的句子必须比第 1 部分答案的句型更复杂。要将这些复杂的句子串在一起，成为一个段落，有整体感。或者说，考官要考察的是考生语言的逻辑性是否强。

考官也要通过第 3 部分来考核考生的英语表达能力上限，从而为考生定档定分。比如考官可能已经从第 1、2 部分发现考生能获得 6 分以上，但是到底是该给 6.5 还是 7 分，就要通过第 3 部分来定夺了。因此经常在第 3 部分会碰到越来越难的题目，这是好事，意味着考官可能给你更高的分数。比如，考官问了一个很难的问题，你答得非常漂亮，那么考官就会把你的档定得更高，可能会超过 7 分。

值得强调的是，问题难不是坏事，考生也不必担心，只有有难度的题目，才能让考生发挥出应有的水平。就像打乒乓球一样，对手越是强大，越能促使自己发挥出更高的水平。如果考官的问题很难，考生也能听懂，并能恰当作答，分数自然很高；万一考官问题太难，甚至听都听不懂，也可以用自己的方式问清再答。能用英语把自己不知道的东西问清楚也是英语水平的体现。

用英语讨论问题的能力。第 1 部分是快节奏的问答，考官不会对考生的答案给出任何评价和反馈。第 2 部分也只是给出 1～2 个小问题，只有在第 3 部分才会有真正意义的讨论。

因此考生不能只是回答考官的问题，考官的问题只是一个个讨论的开始，考生必须在作答之后继续深入讨论。

第 3 部分的问题是环环相扣、互相关联的。当然考官也会有意地突然转向，换个话题，来考察考生对不同话题或者同一个话题不同方面和层面的讨论。

尽管考官手中持有固定的第 3 部分的问题，但考官经常临时改变问题的问法。

第 1 部分的问题往往是关于考生个人，而第 3 部分的问题大部分是关于考生对一些社会问题的个人看法。因而在回答的时候最好不要以个人的情况来开头。要先从宏观层面给出答案，然后可以通过自身情况来进一步说明。

第 3 部分的问题比较抽象、概括。有时候第 3 部分的问题就像写作中的第 2 部分一样。高分的答案如果写下来也就是一篇小作文。

正如前面提到的一样，第 3 部分的考点主要有 7 个，他们是：explaining，giving information，speculating，giving opinions and reasons，suggesting，comparing & contrasting，justifying or defending your opinion。下面就分别汇总了第 3 部分最常考的问题。

Explaining

1. How does having many cars in a city affect the environment?
2. Some people feel nervous before they give a public speech, even after they have had a lot of time to prepare for the speech. Can you suggest why?
3. Why do you think people in different age groups like different kinds of music?
4. Is there any relationship between people's culture and the kind of music they listen to?
5. What are the benefits of music for (young) children?
6. How do children benefit by sharing their toys with other kids?
7. Sometimes the interpretation of history changes over time. Can you suggest any reasons why that happens?
8. What do you think is the value of teaching history in school?
9. What are the pros and cons of having a library that is free?
10. What do you think are the positive and the negative aspects of advertisements in our lives?
11. What are some of the problems that people can have when they have many children?
12. How do you think changes in technology (electronic technology) have affected people's everyday lives?
13. Why do (many) people today move from rural to urban areas?
14. Why do you think many people today are isolated from their neighbours?
15. Why do children need to play with other children?
16. What do you think is the value of holding international conferences?
17. What would be the advantages of having a common global language?
18. Some people think that being interested in hobbies is a waste of time. Can you suggest why these people say that?
19. Why do people like reading magazines?
20. In your opinion, what is a 'healthy diet' and what is an 'unhealthy diet'?
21. What are the reasons for water shortages in (parts of) China?
22. Can you think of any examples of (advanced) technology that are not good for society (or not good for humanity)?
23. Why do you think some people like to do these extreme sports?
24. What do you think is "true happiness"?
25. Why do you think some people who have a lot of money are still not happy?
26. What are some reasons why some people are unhappy in their work?
27. Many (old or older) people feel that their childhood was the happiest (or the best) time of their lives? Can you suggest why they might feel that way?
28. What impact does the use of credit cards have on individual people and on society as a whole?
29. Why do you think supermarkets are becoming more popular in China?

30. Why does receiving a letter make people feel happy?

Giving information

1. What impact do you think traffic jams have on society (or on people)?
2. In what ways do you think decisions made by government affect how much traffic congestion there is? (e.g. town planning/major event planning)
3. What are some of the things that people do that are harmful to their health?
4. Why is unhealthy living on the increase?
5. What are the consequences of an unhealthy lifestyle?
6. What did you learn in schools about health?
7. What has the government (in your country) done to promote a healthy lifestyle among the people?
8. Do you think it's a good idea for employers to encourage their employees to live a healthy life? How can employers do that?
9. What qualities should public speakers have (in order to speak well in public)?
10. What historical places in China would you recommend foreigners visit?
11. Can you suggest any way to make historic sites more attractive (or interesting) for those people who are not very interested in visiting these places?
12. What particular facilities do you think a library should have for children and what particular facilities should it have for old people?
13. What benefits can children get from using libraries?
14. How libraries changed in the past few decades?
15. At the moment in China, what sorts of products are advertised (on TV) the most?
16. What do you think is the role (or the purpose) of advertisements?
17. What (personal) qualities do you think teachers should have?
18. How have cell-phones changed people's lives?
19. How have communication methods in China changed in the past 20 or 30 years?
20. What changes can people control and what changes do we have no control over?
21. In the past 20 or 30 years, have there been any changes in family life (or the family structure) in China?
22. What would you say are the essential facilities (or the important facilities) and services that people need in their town or city?
23. What are some of the typical problems that exist in cities?
24. What electrical appliances are generally used in homes in China?
25. How has modern science and technology changed the way people work in the past generation (20～30 years)?
26. What sorts of films do you think are unsuitable for children to watch?
27. (In China), what factors influence people's choice about what career to enter?

28. What are the most popular leisure time activities in your country?
29. On what occasions (or when) do people in China have a party?
30. In China, what are examples of important events that people celebrate?

Speculating

1. Do you think the problem of traffic congestion will be eased (or solved) in the future or will it become worse?
2. In the future, do you think there will be fewer libraries because of the use of advanced technology?
3. In the future, do you think the internet will become even more important in education? (Why?/How?)
4. With the increasing use of computers for communication, what do you think the eventual result might be?
5. Do you think the skill of handwriting might one day (more or less) disappear?
6. What sorts of problems do you think cities will face in the future?
7. What do you think will be the future development of electronic devices?
8. What do you think electrical or electronic home appliances in the home will be like in the future?
9. What kinds of magazines do you think will be the most popular in the next 20 or 30 years?
10. Do you think modern technology might one day mean there will be no need for business trips?
11. Do you think there will be a greater demand for water in the future?
12. In the future, do you think there will be any changes in the way old people are helped?
13. Do you think the importation of some foreign culture will have an effect on traditional Chinese culture?
14. Do you think radio and television might be replaced by some other medium in the future?
15. In the future, do you think more people will get their news from the Internet?
16. Do you think small shops might disappear in the future? (Why?/Why not?)
17. Do you think the growing number of supermarkets will have any negative effect on society?
18. Do you think e-books will replace the way we read now?

Giving opinion and reasons

1. Which vehicles are more likely to be in traffic jams, cars or buses?
2. Why do so many people want to own their own car?
3. Do you think it's only the responsibility of the government to solve this problem (and not the responsibility of ordinary people)?
4. Do you think having more public transportation is the answer to traffic congestion?

5. Do you think building more roads (motorways (freeways)/highways) will solve the problem?
6. Overseas, some governments have increased the sales tax on cars as a way to discourage people from buying cars. Do you think that's a good idea?
7. Do you think big and small cars should be taxed the same amount (sales tax when buying) ?
8. More and more people in today's society are overweight. Why do you think this is happening?
9. Do you think the government should bring in a law, (similar to banning smoking in certain places), to compel people to do more exercise?
10. Who do you think has the greatest responsibility for educating children about health – parents or schools?
11. Do you think employers have a responsibility to ensure that their employees have a safe and healthy work environment?
12. Do you think listening to (speeches and) lectures is important?
13. Do you think the influence of Western music in China has been a negative or a positive influence?
14. What do you think of giving expensive toys to children?
15. Do you think it would be good if modern computer games replace toys?
16. Do you think students and retired people should have to pay to enter a historic site?
17. Do you think that people are (or should be) responsible for looking after their parents when the parents are old?
18. At what age do you think children should start to have a sense of responsibility towards their communities?
19. Do you think communication between nations can help to avoid war?
20. Who do you think should be responsible for deciding what films children can and cannot watch, parents or the government?
21. Do you think it would be suitable for university students in China to study part-time and also do part-time work at the same time?
22. Some parents think that their children should spend all of their time on study and no time on leisure activities. Do you agree?
23. Do you think the protection of water resources should be a national concern or an international one?
24. Who do you think should finance (i.e.pay for) scientific research, government or private companies?
25. Do you think new scientific knowledge should be freely shared (or made available for others, including the public) or are there situations when it is suitable to not share new scientific knowledge?
26. Do you think the government should restrict (or ban) some of these extreme sports?
27. Some professional athletes have an extremely high income. What's your opinion of this?

28. Would you say happy people work better?
29. Do you think old people should work?
30. Do you think there should be a set age at which people must retire from work?
31. Who do you think should take care of old people, families or the government?

Suggesting

1. What would you suggest as possible solutions to the problem of congested traffic?
2. What things do you think people in China need to do (or need to change) in order to improve their health?
3. Can you suggest some ways for a person to lose weight?
4. What could the government do to help people quit smoking?
5. Can you suggest how classical music could be made more attractive for young people?
6. Nowadays, a lot of shops (and other businesses) play background music in their shops. Can you suggest why they do that?
7. How can people get information about historic sites?
8. What restrictions do you think should be applied to the advertising industry?
9. How can we solve the problem of children seeing these advertisements?
10. Ideally, what roles do you think men and women should play in a family? FQ
11. Besides taking a course, what other ways are there for people to learn things?
12. How do you think universities could help students to find work after they graduate?
13. If you were the government, what changes would you bring about in society?
14. Do you think the educational system in China needs any changes? (What changes? Why?/Why not?)
15. What do you think the government could do to improve the living situation in the countryside?
16. How do you think the facilities in your hometown could be improved?
17. Can you suggest some ways that the film industry could use to attract a larger audience to their films?
18. If someone has little (or no) free time for leisure activities, what do you suggest they do?
19. Can you suggest some ways to help preserve traditional leisure time activities in your culture?
20. Can you suggest any way to make traditional food more attractive? (more attractive for people to eat or buy)
21. What would you suggest we do to overcome the problem of water shortage?
22. How can (or could) people be made more aware of these problems?
23. What are some ways people can (or could) protect themselves when they do dangerous sporting activities?
24. Can you think of any way to improve the help that people in the community get?

25. Can you suggest any way for people to help themselves have a good memory?
26. How do you think children could be encouraged to read more?
27. Can you suggest how old people could find work (that is suitable for them)?
28. Some old people are very lonely. Can you suggest any way to help them feel less lonely?
29. If you were planning a new city, what factors would you consider?
30. Can you suggest any way that we could reduce the noise in the cities?
31. How do you think China's postal system could be improved?

Comparing and contrasting

1. What are the advantages and disadvantages of emails compared to handwritten letters?
2. Compare the way old people and young people spend their leisure time.
3. Do men and women like to read the same kinds of things?
4. Compare the importance of practical skills and academic skills.
5. Compare the value of knowledge gained from books to knowledge gained from practical experience in the workplace.
6. Compare the way men spend their leisure time and the way women spend their leisure time.
7. Compare photos taken by professional photographers and typical family photos.
8. Compare listening to the radio to watching TV.
9. Do men and women have the same attitudes towards gift giving?
10. Do old people and young people like doing the same kinds of things outdoors?
11. Do young people and old people have the same attitudes towards advertisements?
12. Do men and women have the same buying habits when they buy clothes?
13. Compare books and movies as media for showing history.
14. Do women and men like to watch the same kinds of TV programs?
15. Compare reading books and watching movies. Which can you learn more from? How?/Why?
16. If you had to choose one of two different jobs, one being well-paid but not interesting and the other poorly-paid but interesting, which job would you choose?
17. Do you prefer watching films at home or in a cinema?
18. Are boys and girls interested in the same games or play activities?
19. Are there any differences between the games boys like to play and those girls like to play?
20. Compare modern weddings in China with traditional Chinese weddings.

Justifying or defending your opinion

1. Why do you think every child should learn swimming?
2. You said we should limit the number of cars. Can you explain it a little bit?
3. I can't agree with you on… would you give me an example?
4. Some people are crazy shoppers and never save money. Why do you think they do this?
5. Why do you think going overseas is the best way to learn a foreign language?

第二周　7天基础：做透7套真题

本周学习目标

本周是雅思口语学习的第二周。在本周的学习过程中，我们将会完整地做7套口语真题。在学习这些真题的基础之上，深入透彻地了解雅思口语考试第1部分的常考话题。从而全面掌握回答第1部分问题必须具备的语言基础。

每天学习内容的安排是：

1. **真题及自测评分表**：一套完整的雅思口语考试真题。建议考生自问自答（如果能找到提问的考官更佳）并录音，在回答完一套真题后，听录音，以考官的角度，给自己一个评分。自己听录音非常重要，从中能听出很多明显的错误，这样能使自己印象深刻，僻免下次再犯。另外，反复给自己评分，可以更加深刻地理解评分标准，做到心中有数。
2. **模板答案**：在自己评分之后，可以学习这套真题的模板答案。从模板答案中吸取养分，补充自测中的不足。
3. **深度透析真题话题**：学完模板答案后，就是对这套真题中涉及的话题的深入分析，学些话题词汇、表达法和答题思路。
4. **拓展问题**：除了真题中出现的问题以外，与这些话题相关的、常考的其他问题也会被列举出来，以便考生学习。

本周学习目录

星期三	The Introduction	
	Part 1	Topic 1 Computer and Internet Topic 2 News Topic 3 Weather
	Part 2	Topic 4 Describe something you do that is good for your health
	Part 3	Topic 5 A healthy lifestyle Topic 6 People's health
星期四	The Introduction	
	Part 1	Topic 1 Advertisements Topic 2 Friends Topic 3 Flowers
	Part 2	Topic 4 Describe a success you would like to achieve (in the near future)
	Part 3	Topic 5 Success Topic 6 Competition
星期五	The Introduction	
	Part 1	Topic 1 Art Topic 2 Plans and goals Topic 3 Time
	Part 2	Topic 4 Describe an important letter that you received
	Part 3	Topic 5 Handwritten letters Topic 6 Letters in the business world
星期六	The Introduction	
	Part 1	Topic 1 Birthdays Topic 2 Birds Topic 3 Holidays
	Part 2	Topic 4 Describe a TV program that you watched but didn't like
	Part 3	Topic 5 Television tastes Topic 6 TV stars
星期日	The Introduction	
	Part 1	Topic 1 Emails Topic 2 Noise Topic 3 Swimming
	Part 2	Topic 4 Describe a change you would like to make to your life in the future
	Part 3	Topic 5 People's feelings about change Topic 6 Personal change

星期一

第一套真题

一、真题及自测评分表

The Introduction (25 to 30 seconds)

1. Good morning/afternoon. My name is______. Can you tell me your full name, please?
2. What shall I call you?
3. Can you tell me where you're from?
4. Can I see your identification, please?

Part 1 (4 to 5 minutes)

Topic 1 Work & studies

1. Do you work or are you a student?
2. What kind of job do you do/ what do you study?
3. Why do you choose that job/ why do you choose that subject?
4. What kind of job do you want to do in future?

Topic 2 Reading

1. Do you like reading?
2. What sorts of things do you most often (or usually) read?
3. Where do you usually do your reading?
4. What are the differences between what you read (and how you read) today, compared to when you were a child?

Topic 3 Food and cooking

1. Can you cook? What can you cook?
2. Who usually does the cooking in your family?
3. Do you usually eat at home or do you usually eat away from home (i.e. "eat out")?
4. Do you think everyone should learn how to cook?

Part 2 (3 to 4 minutes)

Topic 4

Describe a course you would like to take (in the future), if you have time. You should say:

> what (kind of) course it is
> where you would do this course
> what you would like to learn in this course
> how easy or difficult you think it would be
> and explain how you would benefit from taking this course.

wrap-up questions:

1. Do you think you really will do this course?
2. Are there many schools in China that have that course?

Part 3 (4 to 5 minutes)

Topic 5 The value of different kinds of courses

1. Do you think school lessons and teachers are necessary for successful learning?
2. Do you think there are any courses (or subjects) that don't contribute much to China's development?
3. Do you think elective courses (elective subjects) in high school or university are very useful?
4. What are the most popular courses (i.e. subjects, majors) that people study today (at university or other tertiary educational institutes) in China? (Why?)

Topic 6 Continuing education

1. Do you think learning should be a part of everyday life or should there be a time when people stop learning?
2. When people in the workplace need some extra training or study, whose responsibility do you think it is, the employer's responsibility or the responsibility of the employees?
3. What do you think are some differences between adult education and children's education?
4. How important do you think refresher courses are?

自测评分表

Marking criteria	Band
Fluency and Coherence	
Lexical Resource	
Grammatical Range and Accuracy	
Pronunciation	
Final band (Average score)	

二、模板答案

The Introduction (25 to 30 seconds)

1. Good morning/afternoon. My name is______. Can you tell me your full name, please?

— Good morning/afternoon.

— My name is Zhangsan.

2. **What shall I call you?**

— Please call me by my English name Peter/Mary.

3. **Can you tell me where you're from?**

— I'm from Shandong Province.

4. **Can I see your identification, please?**

— Yes, here you are.

Part 1 (4 to 5 minutes)

Topic 1 Work & studies

1. **Do you work or are you a student?**

— I am a student, studying in Beijing Normal University, which is the best teachers' university in China.

2. **What do you study?**

— I study Computer Science, actually I specialize in Internet Engineering.

3. **Why do you choose that subject?**

— Well, first of all, you know I was quite interested in computer games when I was in middle school. Also, I was told that Computer Science would be the most popular subject in the 21st century.

4. **What kind of job do you want to do in the future?**

— Well, I really want to be an internet engineer in a big company, so that I can use all the knowledge that I am learning now.

Topic 2 Reading

1. **Do you like reading?**

— Yes, I do. I read almost every day. I like to keep a book in my bag/purse and I read it when I wait for the bus or ride on the subway.

2. **What sorts of things do you most often (or usually) read?**

— I usually read newspapers such as 21st Century which is an English newspaper and Beijing Youth. Besides, I also read magazines, my favorite one is College Students which is a bilingual reading material.

3. **Where do you usually do your reading?**

— I usually do my reading in the classroom where I can concentrate better. I also often read when I wait for a bus or ride on a subway. In addition, I like to do a bit of reading while lying in bed before I sleep in the evenings.

4. **What are the differences between what you read (and how you read) today, compared to when you were a child?**

— Today I read newspapers, magazines, novels and so on, and I read some of them on the Internet. Whereas in contrast I read pictures and picture-story books while I was a child.

Topic 3 Food and cooking

1. Can you cook? What can you cook?

— Yes, I can cook. But I don't cook well. I can cook noodles and rice. For dishes, I can do tomatoes and eggs and fried potatoes. Also, I can do salad which is very easy. All you need to do is to mix up the vegetables, or fruits and the dressings.

2. Who usually does the cooking in your family?

— In most families, it's the mothers who do the cooking, and this is true in my family. My mom is a good cook. She is good at cooking a variety of cuisines. For instance, Chuan dishes, Cantonese dishes, even western dishes.

3. Do you usually eat at home or do you usually eat away from home (i.e. "eat out")?

— I usually eat at home. I worry about the hygiene problem when I eat out. Also, homemade foods and dishes fit my appetite the best, especially the comfort food. Additionally, eating home is more economical than eating out in a restaurant.

4. Do you think everyone should learn how to cook?

— I think everyone should learn how to cook as a basic living skill, at least, we need to learn how to boil water, how to cook noodles, or rice, how to make a Hamburg or sandwich, and how to make a salad. These are basic cooking yet they are important as they are essential for daily life.

Part 2 (3 to 4 minutes)

Topic 4

Describe a course you would like to take (in the future), if you have time.

You should say:

what (kind of) course it is

where you would like to do this course

what you would learn in this course

how easy or difficult you think it would be

and explain how you would benefit from taking this course.

If I have time, I think I would like to take a course of English. I have been thinking of polishing my English for a long time because I work in a joint-venture company and I use English almost every work day. For example, to write reports , or to make a presentation in front of my boss who is British. Sometimes there are misunderstandings occurred due to inappropriate use of vocabulary or grammar, which makes me feel incompetent or inferior to those whose English proficiency are excellent. Through a course of English, I would learn vocabulary, grammar as well as phonetics, and this could best improve my weak areas in the use of language. It would be difficult to me when I have to wear two hats at the same time, I mean to take the course while keeping the job. But, I'm strongly motivated as I would improve my language skill which is crucial to my future promotion.

wrap-up questions:

1. Do you think you really will do this course?

— Yes, I think I would.

2. Are there many schools in China that have that course?

— Yes, lots of private-owned schools run that course as their major business, so I have many choices.

Part 3 (4 to 5 minutes)

Topic 5 The value of different kinds of courses

1. Do you think school lessons and teachers are necessary for successful learning?

— Generally speaking, I think school lessons and teachers are necessary for successful learning to young kids who need guidance with learning. They lack experience of learning, and do not know the most effective way to learn. As for adults who have received the type of conventional school education for many years, they can be independent enough to learn themselves through the internet as well as many other resources.

2. Do you think there are any courses (or subjects) that don't contribute much to China's development?

— So far, I haven't found any courses or subjects that don't contribute much to China's development. I think all of the current courses which are available on the school syllabus are essential to the development of China. They are scientifically designed and effectively carried out by China's Ministry of Education.

3. Do you think elective courses (elective subjects) in high school or university are very useful?

— Yes, I think so. Elective courses are the ones chosen by the students themselves. When students decide which elective courses to choose, they have the freedom to choose and to think of their interests. As an old saying goes "interest is the best teacher". I believe that, with the elective courses, the students may not work their best, but they can best enjoy at learning .

4. What are the most popular courses (i.e. subjects, majors) that people study today (at university or other tertiary educational institutes) in China? (Why?)

— Probably Accounting and Business Management are the most popular courses that people study today. People choose to study these two subjects for better job perspectives. In addition, being accountants and business managers are attractive to job hunters as they are decent.

Topic 6: Continuing education

1. Do you think learning should be a part of everyday life or should there be a time when people stop learning?

— I think learning should be a part of everyday life so long as people learn for the sake of learning. When people learn for the sake of learning, they enjoy the pleasure of learning. While in contrast when people learn for practical interests/purposes, for example to gain a degress so as to find a decent or well-paid job, then the fun of learning is usually lessened on that level, and I don't think anyone would enjoy this type of learning on a life-long course.

2. When people in the workplace need some extra training or study, whose responsibility do you think it is, the employer's responsibility or the responsibility of the employees?

— If that extra training or study contributes to the improvement or further development of the company, doubtlessly, it's the employer's responsibility to provide that extra training or study. Yes, it costs the employer's lots of money to train their employees. However, I think a wise employer should see that he earns more profits from their well-trained employees who produce better products or services to the business the company does.

3. What do you think are some differences between adult education and children's education?

— Adult education is profession-oriented whereas children's education is mainly focused on character formation and intelligence developments. Both of these educations involve learning. But adult education is academic. On the contrary, children's education is non-academic and fun.

4. How important do you think refresher courses are?

— I think refresher courses are extremely important. In the imformation age, knowledge is updated quickly. Refresher courses can help people/students keep up with the latest developments.

三、深度透析

（一）个人信息

按照口语考试流程，考官在检查完 ID 后，将进入第一个话题。一般情况下，第一个话题是 your home (house or hometown or home province or home country)或者是 your work /studies。这些问题都属于个人信息。每个考生都要熟练掌握个人信息的英语表达。

Topic 1 Work & studies

1. Do you work or are you a student?

这是一个非常高频的问题，因为这个问题的答案会决定考官后续问题的方向。如果考生是学生，那么考官会继续问考生的学习情况，而不会谈论工作；如果考生是处于工作状态，考官更多地会关注考生的工作以及以前的学习经历。

周计划提示

简单问题不要简单回答

很多学生在回答这个问题的时候会不假思索地说：“I am a student.”考官必然会问：“What do you study/where do you study?”答案也免不了是：“I study linguistics/I study in Beijing Normal University.”等。这样一来，考生所给的句型全都是简单句，而且信息含量

有限，更重要的是没有体现考生主动参与讨论的意愿，必然会给考官留下不好的印象。

那么下面这个答案怎么样呢？“Well, I am a student, studying Applied Linguistics in Beijing Normal University, which is the best teachers' university in China.”这个答案用了一个简单句、一个分词、一个从句，从句型上都属于高分搭配，说起来自然流畅，充分体现了考生的语言交际能力，而且避免了让考官对一个话题的简单追问，应该是一个值得借鉴的句型。提炼成模版句型应该是：“Well, I am a student, studying ______ in ______ university, which is _______.”请根据自己的实际情况把答案补充完整。每个考生的答案都可以不一样。比如：

- Well, I am a student, studying computer science in Peking University, which is the best university in China.
- Well, I am a student, studying economics in Beijing Institute of Technology, which is one of the best universities for technology.

同样的道理，如果你是在工作，也不要只说 I am working; I work as a sales manager 等。也要用类似的结构来回答这个问题。如：

- Well, actually I have been working as a sales manager in an insurance company for about four years.

或者

- Well, I am working as a sales manager in Macrosoft, which is the best software company apart from Microsoft.

有一种情况是既没有工作也不是学生。你可以说：

- Well, actually I have graduated last year, but I did not get a job yet, cos I was thinking of going abroad to further my education so that I can get a better job in the future.

Your work

如果考官确定你有工作，而你在回答上面问题的时候没有给出具体的有关你工作的信息，考官会继续追问如下问题：

2．What job (or what work) do you do?

3．Why did you choose that job (or that kind of work)?

4．How long have you been working?

5．What does your company do?

6．What do you do (in a typical day) at work?

周计划提示

回答问题要具体

在回答这些问题的时候一定要谨记答案信息要具体，不要大而化之，泛泛而谈。如：在回答最后一个问题的时候可以说：

- Well, you know I am a sales manager, so basically what I do at work is try to sell our products, but more specifically, I stay at office and try to contact all my clients by email and telephone, to see if they would buy more of my products or if they could help me to know more potential clients.

如果考官觉得你能回答这些问题，可能会深入地问一些更具体的问题。下面是考官常问的问题和答案：

7. Is your job related to what you studied in university?

— Well, basically, yes, you know I studied computer science in university, and now I am working in a software company. But more specially, no. I studied software designing, but now I sell it.

8. What's the best thing about your job?

— Generally speaking, I quite like my job, and the best thing is that I have a lot of challenges, which forced me to improve myself, therefore I can be more competitive while I am doing my job, and I can communicate with all kinds of people.

9. What's the most difficult part of your job?

— The most difficult part of my job is to find out who are the ones who may possibly need our products. I will have to spend a lot of time and energy to seek them, and sometimes, it seems that you can never find them no matter how much work you do.

10. Would you like to change your job?

— Not really, I like selling things. I may possibly change a company or set up my own company, but I will still do sales, that's what I was born for.

11. Do you need to work with other people at work?

— Sure, I don't think anybody can do well without working with others in modern society. I need very close cooperation with my colleagues.

12. Do you prefer working alone or with others (Why?)

— Working alone might be good, but I still prefer to work with others, because that would make things much easier with everybody contributing to the work. And, it is more relaxing with somebody to communicate with.

13. Do you use computers in your work?

— Yes, I rely on computers actually; you know the first thing I get to my office is to boot my computer so that I can check my email, which would help to decide what to do in that day. And I have to keep myself updated by browsing the webpages.

14. What would be the ideal job for you?

— Well, I don't know. I quite enjoy the work I am doing now. But maybe, it would be nice if I can be self-employed, I mean I can put my ideas into practice.

15. Why are you taking the IELTS test?

— Since I have been working for years, and I would say I have done very well, but I really want to get a degree in economics in Australia, because some experience in another country would contribute a lot to my career development.

Your Studies

如果考官确定你是学生，他/她会问你如下问题：

16. What subject(s) are you studying?

17. **Why did you choose that subject?**

18. **What school (or university) do you go to?**

19. **How is your school (or university)?**

针对学生的问题可能会更多，因为参加雅思的考生大部分还是学生。下面是非常常考的一些问题和答案：

20. **What are your favourite classes/courses/subjects at university/ school?**

如果你是中学生，考官会选择问你最喜欢的科目。要注意的是 P.E.（体育）算不上 study 的科目，建议大家不要选。因为 study 和 learn 是有区别的。前者有研究的含义，是深入学习，而后者往往是学习一门技能，体育项目一般是 learn。除非你是体育专家，研究某个体育项目。对这个问题的回答也有固定的句型：

— Well, actually I like all the classes/ courses/ subjects at university/ school, but my favorite is still_______, because I want to be a________in future…

每个考生都可以用这个句型给出不同的答案。当然后续再补充说明一点会让你的答案更有个性、更好。

21. **What's the most difficult part of your course?**

跟工作一样，考官希望考生能用英语表述自己学习中的难点。这也是出国后生存英语的重要部分，因此是雅思常考的问题。考官不管你的难点是什么，他/她更多地是关注你是如何用英语表述的。所以，在考试的时候大可不必深思到底难点是什么。应该把更多的精力花在句型上，否则会影响回答问题的流畅性，从而影响得分。比如，无论你是学什么的，也无论你的难点是什么，你都可以这样回答：

— Well, the course I am studying now is not really difficult for me, because that is what I am interested in, however, I do think it is very hard to put the theoretical knowledge I learnt into practice, because they seem so different.

当然，你也可以根据自己的实际情况给出更具体的答案，只要能自圆其说，就大可不必太较真。因为有可能你要说的实际情况恰恰是你用英语所不能表达的。所以需要扬长避短，不能让考官发现你的语言漏洞。

22. **In addition to gaining knowledge, what other ways have you benefited from your school/university experience?**

上学无非就是德智体美劳全面发展；学习理论知识、实践技能；学会做人、做事等。因此回答这个问题很容易，只要选择其中一、两项就可以把这个题目答好。

— I think the school experience has been very beneficial to me, apart from the knowledge I have learnt, I have made many friends, who are always ready to help me whenever I need, and the education I get made me a very confident woman…

23. **Do you prefer studying independently (i.e. studying alone) or with others (or in a group)? (Why?)**

— I am a very introvert person, so I much prefer to study by myself, because I like to be quiet and study deeply. Sometimes, I do discuss with classmates though.

— Well, I hate to be alone, I think study with others would help me to study better because I can always communicate with people whenever I have difficulties.

24. Do you think the things you are studying now in school/university will prepare you well for your future work?

— Not really, because generally, university education only help the students to learn some theoretical knowledge, which can not be put into production immediately. I think more practice is necessary. But I guess, the university education would make me a quick learner, so that I can adapt myself quickly if I get a job afterwards.

— Theoretically yes, but I think I will need more practice in the field, I mean I need to put the knowledge I have learnt into practice in real work.

— Sure, you know I want to be an internet engineer, which is what I am studying now. The university has very good faculty and adequate facilities, so I can learn both theoretical knowledge and practical skills in my university.

Your Home (Your Accommodation)

你的居住情况以及你家里的装饰和周围环境都是考官经常关注的话题。而很多考生都对这一部分准备不够充分，被问到的时候也回答不出什么具体内容。下面对常考问题逐一解答。

25. Do you live in a house or a flat?

周计划提示

房子的概念

“房子”一词在英语中的解释往往更加具体，中国人说买房可能是说买了公寓（apartment/flat）或买了洋楼或者别墅（house），当然还有买平房（bungalow）的。所以当考官问起这个问题的时候，很多中国考生有点不知所措。下面给出不同情况的答案，供各位考生选择使用。

- Well, I live in a three bedroom apartment（三居）with my parents.
- Well, actually, I live on campus. I mean I share a dorm with three other roommates, but back home I have a house which is a three-floor building…
- Well, you know I have a very big extended family. There are about fifteen people in my family, so I live in a quadruple yard（四合院）with them.

26. How long have you lived there?

— I have been living there for about 15 years.

— I lived there since I was born.

— Well, let me see, you know I moved there when I was in primary school, so altogether I have lived there for about ten years.

27. Are the transport facilities to your home very good?

— Yes, definitely, there is a bus stop and a subway station just opposite the building I live in, so I can go wherever I want easily. And taxi is everywhere.

28. Is there anything on the walls of your home?

— Well, yes, although most of my family members prefer to have nothing on the wall. We do have some calligraphy works on the wall of the living room, and I have a movie poster in my bedroom.

29. What's your favorite room in your home? (Why?)

— My favorite room? Well, I love all the rooms, but I spend most of the time in my bedroom, that is where I study and enjoy myself.

30. What can you see when you look out of the window of your room?

对于这个问题的答案经常会落于俗套，很多考生会答道：I can see some trees, flowers, cars and so on. 殊不知，这样简单的罗列会给句型结构的分数大打折扣。其实，考官不可能知道你能看见什么，也不介意你会说什么，所以只要能自圆其说，就可以放开地去说。比如：

— Well, since I live on the 23rd floor of a building, so I can see much. In the evening, I can see the beautiful night of Beijing, and I can see the main structures of the Forbidden City.

其答题技巧是：先创设一个情景（住处很高），为后面的发挥作足铺垫，因为住得高，视野就很广，比如可以看到北京的夜景，甚至是紫禁城等。听到这样的答案，考官肯定比听到你罗列一些名词感兴趣得多。

Your Hometown

31. Where do you come from?

请根据前一部分对这个问题的回答，将下列答案补充完整。

— Well, I am/ come from the city of____________in___________province, which is in_____________, actually, my hometown is famous for___________.

32. Where do you live at the moment?

— Right now, I live on campus, I share a dorm with four boys.

— Now, I live in a three-bedroom apartment with my parents in Haidian District, Beijing.

注意：尽量不要重复考官的问题，如问题中的 at the moment，可以换作 right now, now 等近义词或词组。另外，住在校内，用 live on campus，而不是 live in campus。自然住在校外也就该用 live off campus 了。

33. Do you like living here/there?

回答好恶的问题切忌只用 yes/no, I (don't) like it. 一定要注意句型的多样性。比如可以说：sure, definitely, not really, actually not, frankly speaking, I don't 等词组来开头。

如：

— Not really, it is very comfortable to live there, though. I really want to have some freedom and privacy, because you know my parents take care of every detail of my life, which makes me feel uneasy.

34. Have you ever thought about moving to live somewhere else? (Why?/Why not?)

— Yes, ever since I entered university, because that is the time I started to have my own friends, and especially when I get a boy friend, I don't want to live with my parents any more, you know, in China, parents are just too considerate.

35. What kind of place is your hometown (or the place your are living in now)?

— My hometown is a small city with beautiful scenery, and wherever you go, it is only a walking distance, so it is a very comfortable place to live in.

36. Do you prefer to live in a big city or in the countryside?

— Well, I love the quiet countryside, but I much prefer to live in a big city, because I was born in the city. I am just accustomed to city life. It seems impossible for me to make a living in the countryside.

37. Has your hometown changed much in the past few years?

— Yes, it has been changed a lot, actually I can see the changes taking place in every aspect, for example, ten years ago, there were not so many skyscrapers and luxury cars. I still remember, at that time many people used animals such as donkeys for transportation, but now we have very developed public transportation system.

38. What's the traffic situation like in your hometown (or where you are living now)?

— The traffic is very developed now, apart from the bus system, which takes you to wherever you want to go. Recently, there is a very cleverly designed subway system in operation, which makes our lives much easier, but sometimes, we do have traffic jams.

39. Is there anything you don't like about your hometown?

— Well. Generally speaking, I love my hometown, but the only thing that I can think of which needs improving is that we don't have enough green areas. You know the city is being developed quickly. There are always new roads and buildings being built, but fewer trees have been planted accordingly.

Topic 2 Reading

1. Do you like reading?

可以这样回答：

— Not really.

— Yes, it is one of my favorites.

— Yes, I take it as a hobby.

— Actually, I don't, but I may read some books for special purposes.

2. What do you usually read?

周计划提示

相关词汇

- daily, weekly, semimonthly, monthly, quarterly
- *China Daily, Beijing Review, 21st Century, Overseas' English, English Salon*
- *Times*《泰晤士报》, *Economist*《经济学人》, *Guardian*《卫报》, *National Geographic*《国家地理》, *New Scientist, Science Magazine, US Today, The New York Times*
- cartoon, fairytales, fiction, nonfiction, science and fantasy fiction, biography, love story, detective novel, romance

可以这样回答：

— Well, I read a large amount of materials, such as newspapers, magazines, fictions and novels, among which, I like novels best, because I can enjoy the interesting plot, and learn a lot from the stories happened on the dramatis personae. It can broaden my horizon, enrich my experience and improve the reading comprehension, but it may result in insufficient physical exercise, or degraded eyesight.

Topic 3 Food and cooking

周计划提示

食物

中国独特的传统饮食

馄饨	wonton
锅贴	guotie (fried jiaozi/ Chinese dumpling)
花卷	steamed twisted rolls
套餐	set meal
盒饭	box lunch; Chinese take-away
米豆腐	rice tofu
冰糖葫芦	a stick of sugar-coated haws (or apples, etc.)
火锅	chafing dish
八宝饭	eight-treasure rice pudding
豆腐脑	jellied bean curd

中国菜的英文翻译公式

中国饮食文化博大精深，是世界任何国家所不能匹敌的。很多东西都是中国独有，中国菜的命名更是讲究色香味俱全，让人听起来就有想吃的冲动。因此翻译菜谱也是艺术，很多菜名几乎是不可译的。但在不可或缺的时候，只好退而求其次，将菜的意思翻译出来，好歹让“老外”能知道是个什么东西。在口语表达中，更是要做到达意，这里有一个“万能”公式，可以帮考生翻译几乎所有的中国菜。

烹饪方式+主要原料（或者是荤菜）+ with 配料（或者是素材）

如：

青椒肉丝	fried pork with green pepper
宫爆鸡丁	fried chicken with cucumber
土豆炖牛肉	stewed beef with potato

常见烹饪方法

煮	boil
炖	stew
蒸	steam
炒，烧	fry
炸	deep fry
熏	smoke
烤	roast

常用荤菜	
猪肉	pork
牛肉	beef
羊肉	mutton
其他肉类直接用动物名	
兔子肉	rabbit
鸡肉	chicken
鱼肉	fish
狗肉	dog
羊羔肉	lamb
常用蔬菜	
大白菜	chinese cabbage
马铃薯	potato
胡萝卜	carrot
洋葱	onion
芹菜	celery
紫色包心菜	red cabbage
黄瓜	cucumber
蕃茄	tomato
小萝卜	radish
白花菜	cauliflower
小葱	spring onions
大蒜	garlic
姜	ginger
青椒	green Pepper
红椒	red pepper
黄椒	yellow pepper
蘑菇	mushroom
绿花菜	broccoli florets
四季豆	dwarf Bean
长形平豆	flat Beans
莴苣	lettuce
蕃薯	sweet potato
菠菜	spinach
豌豆	peas
常见西餐名称	
自助餐	Western buffet
冷菜	cold dish

沙拉	salad
冷烤里脊	cold roast fillet
鸡蛋鲱鱼泥子	minced herring with eggs
沙丁油鱼	sardines
鱼肉冻	fish jelly
红鱼子酱	red caviar
黑鱼子酱	black caviar
大虾泥	minced prawns
清汤	light soup
浓汤	thick soup
牛尾汤	ox-tail soup
牛肉丸子汤	beef balls soup
鱼汤	fish soup
洋葱汤	onion soup
鱼排	fish steak
通心粉煮鸡	boiled chicken with macaroni
黄油汁煎鸭肝	fried duck liver with butter sauce
红焖里脊	braised fillet
洋葱软炸里脊片	soft fried fillet slices with onion
牛肉扒	beef steak
咖哩牛肉	curry beef
通心粉红焖牛肉	braised beef with macaroni
炸牛舌	fried ox tongue
法式猪排	pork chop a la France
烤叉烧	barbecued pork
通心粉	macaroni
意式面条	spaghetti
麦片粥	oatmeal porridge
奶酪烤面包片	cheese toast
无黄油烤面包片	dry toast
黑面包	black bread
裸麦面包	rye bread
死面面包	unleavened bread
法式面包	French bread
小圆面包	bun
热狗	hot dog
法式小面包	French roll
三明治	sandwich

馅饼	pie
苹果饼	apple pie, apple tart
巧克力饼	chocolate pie
牛肉饼	minced beef cutlet
水果面包布丁	fruit and bread pudding
甜点心	dessert
炸果饼	fritter
水果冻	fruit jelly
松饼	puff pastry

四、拓展问题

Reading

1. Which do you prefer reading, magazines or newspapers?
2. Do you think reading foreign magazines and newspapers can help you learn a new language?
3. Do you like reading online?
4. What are the benefits and drawbacks of reading online?
5. Will books be replaced by online materials?

Fruits and Vegetables

1. Do you like to eat fruit(s) and vegetables?
2. Do you think people should eat more fruits and vegetables?
3. How much fruit and vegetables do you think a person needs to stay healthy?
4. (In China,) is there much difference between the fruits and vegetables that people eat today and what they used to eat in the past?

Writing

1. Do you often write things?
2. What do you usually write?
3. Do you think computers might one day replace handwriting?
4. When do children begin to write in your country?
5. Do you think handwriting is very important (nowadays)?

星期二

第二套真题

一、真题及自测评分表

The Introduction (25 to 30 seconds)

1. Good morning/afternoon. My name is______. Can you tell me your full name, please?
2. What shall I call you?
3. Can you tell me where you're from?
4. Can I see your identification, please?

Part 1 (4 to 5 minutes)

Topic 1 Leisure time

1. What do you do in your free time? (or What do you do with your friends in your leisure time?)
2. What kinds of leisure time activities are popular with young people today?
3. Do you think modern people like to get together with others?

Topic 2 Clothes

1. Do you like shopping for clothes?
2. What kinds of clothes do you like to wear (or buy)?
3. Do you like to try on clothes before you buy them? (Why?/Why not?)
4. Where do you think you can buy the most fashionable clothes?

Topic 3 Transportation

1. Do you drive a car?
2. Do you often use public transportation?
3. What forms of transportation do you have where you live (in your hometown)?
4. Do you think children should be allowed to drive a car? (Why?/Why not?)

Part 2 (3 to 4 minutes)

Topic 4

Describe a job you think you would be good at. You should say:

what job it would be what would be your typical activities in this job how would you get this job how this work would be different to your current situation and explain why you think you would be able to do this job well.

wrap-up questions:

- Do you know anyone who is doing this job?

Part 3 (4 to 5 minutes)

Topic 5 Choosing a career

1. (In China), what factors influence people's choice when they decide what work to do?
2. Do you think money matters very much when it comes to choosing what work (or job) to do?
3. Where can (or do) young people get help (or get information) when making their choices about their future careers?
4. Do you think it should be one of the responsibilities of schools to provide information (and guidance) about careers?

Topic 6 Work experience

1. In what ways do you think what you are studying now is different to the work you will be doing in the future?
2. Do you think work experience should be included in the high school curriculum (and included in university courses)?
3. How do you think high schools could set up a program to help students gain some practical work experience?
4. Do you think it would be suitable for university students in China to study part-time and also do part-time work, at the same time?

自测评分表

Marking criteria	Band
Fluency and Coherence	
Lexical Resource	
Grammatical Range and Accuracy	
Pronunciation	
Final band (Average Score)	

二、模板答案

The Introduction (25 to 30 seconds)

1. Good morning/afternoon. My name is_______. Can you tell me your full name, please?

— My name is Li Si.

2. **What shall I call you?**

— I have an English name, Bill. So please just call me Bill.

3. **Can you tell me where you're from?**

— I'm from Beijing.

4. **Can I see your identification, please?**

— Yes, please.

Part 1 (4 to 5 minutes)

Topic 1 Leisure time

1. **What do you do in your free time? (or What do you do with your friends in your leisure time?)**

— In my free time, I do some reading and listen to music. If time is convenient for both my friends and me, we'll find some time to hang out.

2. **What kinds of leisure time activities are popular with young people today?**

— There are several kinds of leisure time activities that are popular with young people today such as surfing on the Internet, watching movies, listening to music, reading, doing some shopping, bicycling, mountain-climbing, fishing, doing some sports and so on. We can see that life for young people today can be so fun.

3. **Do you think modern people like to get together with others?**

— Yes. Some modern people feel that the advanced modern communication such as mobile phones as well as Internet alienate people. The more time people spend in communicating through mobile text messages or e-mailing, the more time people spend alone and thus feel loneliness. From this perspective, I think modern people like to get together with others, which means communicating face-to-face.

— No. With the modern way of communicating, people can communicate through mobile phones and Internet with which they feel freer to express their opinions and emotions and not worrying about being embarrassed as much as they feel at face-to-face communication. Under this circumstances, I don't think modern people like to get together with others. Instead, they prefer to spend time alone and enjoy their personal life in a very individual way.

Topic 2 Clothes

1. **Do you like shopping for clothes?**

— Well, I don't very much like shopping for clothes. As fashion/clothes styles updates too fast and it's not easy to keep up with the up-to-minute fashion. Plus, fashionable clothes are often expensive. So I am not very keen on spending a fortune on something that doesn't stay in trend for long.

2. **What kinds of clothes do you like to wear (or buy)?**

— I like to wear casual clothes. Most casual clothes are made of material of cotton, which makes skin comfortable. Also, they are usually made loose, which enables free movements of the body.

3. Do you like to try on clothes before you buy them? (Why?/Why not?)

— Yes, definitely. Unless you try on clothes before you buy them, you can be assured that your purchase is correct. Otherwise, you take the risk of buying the wrong size or inappropriate style or color.

4. Where do you think you can buy the most fashionable clothes?

— I think I can buy the most fashionable clothes in the exclusive shops. Clothes sold in that kind of shops are usually extraordinarily expensive. They are unique in style and pattern and color. To some extent, they are not purely clothes. They are a symbol of status as well.

Topic 3 Transportation

1. Do you drive a car?

— No, I don't. I have passed the examination of driving license but I have never intended to do the real driving. I live in a city where a variety of transportation is available and the mass public transportation is quite cheap. Plus, the worsened traffic congestion and environment pollution, I just don't want to buy a car to drive. I hope more people can think like I do, thus each individual can contribute a little to the kind of green life we once lived but now have lost.

2. Do you often use public transportation?

— Yes. Always. From what I have just mentioned to you, Mr. Examiner, I don't drive a car, and I use public transportation whenever I travel.

3. What forms of transportation do you have where you live (in your hometown)?

— In my city, the forms of transportation are various such as subway, taxi, buses. For long distance travel, vans/coaches, trains, aeroplanes are all available. Most of these forms of transportation provides good service. They are convenient and comfortable. Sometimes some of them can be expensive though.

4. Do you think children should be allowed to drive a car? (Why?/Why not?)

— No, I don't think children should be allowed to drive a car. It is simply because of danger. Just think of the car accident rate which has been rising year by year and the fact that only adults are allowed to drive based on the law. This means even an adult who is supposed to be physically and mentally mature enough to have self-control sometimes ignore the traffic disciplines, for example, to drive after drinking or drive at excessive speed or high-risk maneuvers such as overtaking dangerously or driving when tired, all of which plays a major role in most fatal traffic accidents. Then shall we allow the children who are physically and mentally less mature than adults thus having insufficient discretion to drive?

Part 2 (3 to 4 minutes)

Topic 4

Describe a job you think you would be good at. You should say: what job it would be

what would be your typical activities in this job how would you get this job how this work would be different to your current situation and explain why you think you would be able to do this job well.

I think the job would be to take a group of people to travel, that is, to be a tour guide. I would greet the traveling groups with a smiling face, and I would tell them stories with emotions and passions as well as humors about those historical sites and beautiful landscapes we would visit. I would also do some fun/exciting team activities to stir up the travelers if they would get tired due to traveling during the journey. All in all, I would do my best to make the journey a lovely one to anyone who would travel with me. I would generate a marvelous memory to the visitors not only for that journey but also a memory which would bring smiling back on their faces one more time again many years later. I would feel self-fulfilled if it would be so. Actually, I think it would be so because I would be able to do this job well as I enjoy traveling and love meeting new people. To me, it's fun to get around with people of different characters and cultural backgrounds.

wrap-up questions:

- **Do you know anyone who is doing this job?**

  — Yes, I do. One of my friends is a tour guide and she has made friends coming from more than twenty countries.

Part 3 (4 to 5 minutes)

Topic 5 Choosing a career

1. (In China), what factors influence people's choice when they decide what work to do?

— Basically, people consider the salary, the working environment and patterns, possibility of getting promotion, holidays, training or further education. Last but not the least, insurance. These are the usual factors which influence people's choice on job decisions, and the factors can be varied according to age, qulifications, abilities and interests of the individuals.

2. Do you think money matters very much when it comes to choosing what work (or job) to do?

— In China, to most people, the answer is "Yes". That's why so many people feel bored with their jobs yet they still try their best to work. Otherwise, they may get fired and have no money to support themselves or their families. Money is not everything. However, almost everything needs money. So I believe to most people, money matters very much when choosing what work to do.

3. Where can (or do) young people get help (or get information) when making their choices about their future careers?

— I think the media such as Internet, newspapers, TV and so on. Besides, their college professors, colleagues, parents, friends can be the source of information on their career choices. I'm trying to think of any organizations where young people in China can get help on this point. Yet personally I don't know any.

4. **Do you think it should be one of the responsibilities of schools to provide information (and guidance) about careers?**

— I agree that it should be one of the responsibilities of schools to provide information (and guidance) about careers. Schools are the place where students are trained and get ready to work in the society. Based on this aspect, schools are supposed to be familiar with what their students can do and what society needs their students to do, which enables the schools to be adequate to provide information (and guidance) about careers. Furthermore, guidance also means to educate, and the essential responsibility of schools are doubtlessly to educate. Thus, I personally agree that providing information (and guidance)on careers should be one of the responsibilities of schools.

Topic 6 Work experience

1. **In what ways do you think what you are studying now is different to the work you will be doing in the future?**

— I think the difference lies between the input and output of the knowledge. What I am studying now is inputting the book knowledge, which is theoretical. Whereas in contrast I will be doing the output of the knowledge at work in the future, which is practical.

2. **Do you think work experience should be included in the high school curriculum (and included in university courses)?**

— Yes, I think work experience should be included in the high school curriculum(and included in university courses). For one thing, there are always differences between theory and practice, that is, book knowledge and practical knowledge. For another thing, work experience helps students develop their personalities, shape up a positive attitude, and hopefully nurse ambitions and gain visions.

3. **How do you think high schools could set up a program to help students gain some practical work experience?**

— High schools could cooperate with organizations and companies in society to develop programs to help students gain some practical work experience. Such programs can be mutually beneficial to both sides. On one hand, the students get job opportunities from which they gain practical work experience, and probably in the mean time to earn some pocket money. On the other hand, the benefits of organizations and companies are the low cost of working force.

4. **Do you think it would be suitable for university students in China to study part-time and also do part-time work at the same time?**

— I think it would be suitable for university students in China to study part-time and also do part-time work at the same time. Generally, syllabuses of universities in China are designed on the basis of giving students plenty of time to develop their own social activities. Students can take that time to do part-time work from which they can gain some work experience and earn some money. So long as they can get a balance between study and work, it would be suitable for them.

三、深度透析

Leisure time

1. What do you do in your free time?

回答这个问题的常用句型：

— Well, normally I'd like to …

— I usually/ always/often …

回答这个问题的话题可以是：

sports, travel, Internet, movie, music, TV, reading, eating, shopping, hobby…

Sample answers:

— Actually I don't have much spare time, but whenever I get some time off, I would…

— Well, in my spare time, I love to invite my friends and have a big meal with them in my favorite restaurant.

— Since I am dreaming to publish my own album, so I often go out with my digital camera to seek some good snaps.

— Frankly speaking, I spend all of my spare time in the Internet cafe, cos I'm really keen on computer games.

— Well, I spent lots of time chatting with my online wife.

— To read some books of my favorite kind is my only choice, cos I am a very quiet person.

— Actually I am a couch potato, I'm so addicted to switching the remote controller of my TV.

— Well, you know I am a student, so I seldom get any spare time, but whenever I get some time off, I would like to go watch a horror movie with my girlfriend, cos she is so crazy about it.

2. What kinds of leisure time activities are popular with young people today?

该题的答题要点可以借鉴第 1 题的内容。如：surfing on line，playing computer games，KTV，shopping 等。并采用“一般到具体”的思路进行回答。如：

— Well, it is hard to say, because there are many activities that are popular among young people, but students often play computer games when they are free, while those who get jobs often go to KTV to release the tension they get from their work.

3. Do you often do things with others in a group (or with your friends)?

第 1 部分的问题往往非常简单。然而问题虽然简单，要答得好也不容易。很多时候考生在面对简单问题的时候也只是草草了事，一个词、一个词组或是一个句子带过。这样做是不合适的。应采用“铺垫+答案+解释”这个公式将话题展开。如：

— Well, you know I am a very introvert person, so I seldom do things with others in a group, I much prefer to do things by myself, because I often feel nervous even uncomfortable to be with others.

下面两个问题同样可以用这个公式来回答。

4. **Do you prefer to go out with your friends or to invite them to your home?**

— Well, since I live with my parents and grandparents, who would never allow me to make too much noise, I prefer to go out with my friends, so that we can have much more fun, without having to listen to my grandma complaining about the noise.

5. **Do you think modern people like to get together with others?**

— Since modern technology makes communication easier, people can contact and communicate with people by using telephone and Internet, which means they don't have to meet each other to get ideas shared and things done. However, this convenience makes people more eager to get together with others, because people also need face-to-face communication. And the less they do, the more they feel they need.

其他话题常用词汇

Clothes

suit	男士西服
dress	女士正装
everyday clothes	便服
three-piece suit	三件套
uniform	制服
overalls	工装裤
rompers	连背心的背带裤
formal dress	礼服
tailcoat, morning coat	大礼服
evening dress	晚礼服
dress coat, tails	燕尾服，礼服
nightshirt	男式晚礼服
dinner jacket	无尾礼服（美语常用 tuxedo）
full dress uniform	礼服制服
frock coat	双排扣长礼服
gown, robe	礼袍
tunic	长袍
overcoat	男式大衣
topcoat	夹大衣
fur coat	皮大衣
three-quarter coat	中长大衣
dust coat	风衣
mantle, cloak	斗篷
sheepskin jacket	羊皮夹克
jacket	短外衣夹克
anorak, duffle coat	带兜帽的夹克，带风帽的粗呢大衣

bathrobe	浴衣
nightgown, nightdress	女睡衣
pyjamas	睡衣裤（美语常用 pajamas）
wing collar	硬翻领，上浆翻领
V-neck	V 型领
sleeve	袖子
T-shirt	短袖圆领衫，T 恤衫
vest	汗衫（美语常用 undershirt）
sweater	运动衫
short-sleeved sweater	短袖运动衫
roll-neck sweater	高翻领运动衫
round-neck sweater	圆领运动衫
twinset	两件套，运动衫裤
kimono	和服
cardigan	开襟毛衣
jeans	牛仔裤
short trousers	短裤
skirt	裙子
divided skirt, split skirt	裙裤
underwear	内衣裤
waistcoat	背心
bathing trunks	游泳裤
boot	靴子
slippers	便鞋
sandal	凉鞋
canvas shoes, rope soled shoes	帆布鞋
clog	木拖鞋
gloves	手套

Transportation

subway, underground, metro	地铁
ferry	轮渡
double Decker	双层巴士

四、拓展问题

Traveling

1. Do you like traveling?
2. What are some places that you have traveled to?
3. What was the last place you traveled to?
4. Which city (or place) that you have been to did you like the most? (Why?)

5. Which country would you like to travel to (in the future)?
6. What places in China would you recommend (or suggest) people visit?
7. Why do you think traveling is so popular nowadays?

Shopping

1. Do you like (going) shopping? (Why?/Why not?)
2. How often do you go shopping?
3. Do you prefer shopping alone or with others?
4. Do you prefer to go shopping with family members or with friends?
5. What time of the day do you prefer to go shopping?
6. What (kinds of) things do you usually buy?
7. Do you prefer to buy things in small shops or in big supermarkets and department stores?
8. Is there anything you dislike about (going) shopping?

Bicycles

1. Do you ever ride a bicycle?
2. What do you use a bicycle for?
3. Would you say it's difficult to learn to ride a bicycle?
4. Did you learn to ride a bicycle when you were a child?
5. What would you say are the advantages of bicycles over cars?
6. Would you say bicycles are suitable for people of all ages?
7. Has the number of bicycle riders in China changed much in the past few years?
8. Do you think the number of people using bicycles (in your hometown/country) will change in the future?

Collecting

1. Do you collect anything as a hobby?
2. Why do you think people like collecting things?
3. If you had a lot of money, what would you like to collect?

星期三

第三套真题

一、真题及自测评分表

The Introduction (25 to 30 seconds)

1. Good morning/afternoon. My name is________. Can you tell me your full name, please?
2. What shall I call you?
3. Can you tell me where you're from?
4. Can I see your identification, please?

Part 1 (4 to 5 minutes)

Topic 1 Computer & Internet

1. Do you use computers very much/ do you often use the Internet?
2. What was your impression (or feeling) when you used a computer the first time?
3. What do you do on the Internet (computer)?
4. What do you think are the benefits of using a computer (the Internet)?

Topic 2 News

1. Are you very interested in the news?
2. How important is it to you to get the news every day?
3. How do you usually find this news?
4. Which do you think is more important, domestic (or local) news or international news?

Topic 3 Weather

1. What's the weather (usually) like in your hometown?
2. What's your favourite weather? (Why?)
3. Do you like snow? (Why?)
4. Does the weather ever affect what you do?

Part 2 (3 to 4 minutes)

Topic 4

Describe something you do that is good for your health. You should say:

what you do when you began to do it how often you do it and explain why you think this is important for your health.

wrap-up questions:

- Would you recommend that to your friends?

Part 3 (4 to 5 minutes)

Topic 5 A healthy lifestyle

1. What are some of the things that people do that are harmful to their health?
2. What do you think are the differences between healthy food and "junk food"?
3. What things do you think people in China need to do (or need to change) in order to improve their health?
4. More and more people in today's society are overweight. Why do you think this is happening?

Topic 6 People's health

1. Do you think the media can play a role in educating people about health? (How?)
2. Do you think doctors have a responsibility to give people advice about how to have a healthy lifestyle?
3. Do you think employers have a responsibility to ensure that their employees have a safe and healthy work environment?
4. Do you think it's a good idea for employers to encourage their employees to live a healthy life? How can employers do that?

自测评分表

Marking criteria	Band
Fluency and Coherence	
Lexical Resource	
Grammatical Range and Accuracy	
Pronunciation	
Final Band (Average Score)	

二、模板答案

The Introduction (25 to 30 seconds)

1. Good morning/afternoon. My name is Peter. Can you tell me your full name, please?

— I'm Tian Wei. Tian is my family name.

2. What shall I call you?

— Please call me Mary.

3. **Can you tell me where you're from?**
   — I'm from Henan Province.
4. **Can I see your identification, please?**
   — Yes, please.

Part 1 (4 to 5 minutes)

Topic 1 Computer & Internet

1. **Do you use computers very much/ do you often use the Internet?**
   — Yes, I do. I use computers almost everyday. Mainly, I use them to check emails and reply emails. Also, I use them a lot to surf on the Internet to get information such as news or sometimes to find solutions about some problems.
2. **What was your impression (or feeling) when you used a computer the first time?**
   — Awesome and Curious! The very first time I used a computer was back in the 1990s, and I was trying to learn how to use emails. When I clicked the button to get the email sent out, and some minutes later, a reply from my friend in America to that email popped up on the screen, I was a kind of stunned "Wow, my God!" Since then, I got addicted to use computers and always wondered what and how I could do more with them.
3. **What do you do on the Internet (computer)?**
   — I write emails, read news, search information on the web, chat online, shop online, watch movies, listen to some music, edit files and pictures. I just can't imagine how I could get through a day without a computer.
4. **What do you think are the benefits of using a computer (the Internet)?**
   — Since computers connect one individual to the world, it opens up a window of possibilities and opportunities. Besides, efficiency and productivity at work and life as well as study are all greatly improved.

Topic 2 News

1. **Are you very interested in the news?**
   — Yes, very much. I love watching any kinds of news programs to get the lastest trend of the world. Some news are exciting while some are sad. Still there are news are unbelievable yet it happens.
2. **How important is it to you to get the news every day?**
   — It's rather important to me to get the news every day. News is dynamic as the world is changing every second. To get the updated news of the world every day enables me feel the pulse of the world, that is, the life of the world.
3. **How do you usually find the news?**
   — I usually find the news through watching TV, reading newspapers as well as surfing on the internet. Among these, I find the news the most often from watching TV.
4. **Which do you think is more important, domestic (or local) news or international news?**
   — I personally think domestic or local news is more important than international news as it is

more influential to local people's daily life. International news is mostly about stories happening in other countries. However, sometimes they can be influential if the news is in a global sense. For example, the news of the breakout of the Financial Tsunami.

Topic 3 Weather

1. What's the weather (usually) like in your hometown?

— The four seasons are very clear in my hometown. In summer, the highest temperature is about 39 degrees. In winter, the lowest temperature is around 17 degrees. It is windy in most of the days during spring and autumn.

2. What's your favourite weather? (Why?)

— I like rainy weather the best. I feel calm and relaxed in this kind of weather. Also, when there are bouts of heavy rains, it cools down the high temperature and gives people a couple of days of respite in a hot summer.

3. Do you like snow? (Why?)

— Yes, I do like snow. For one reason, it is white which stands for purity and holiness. For another reason, snow reminds me of those sweet and cheerful memories of celebrations of the most important festivals of a year such as the the Chinese Spring Festival, the New Year as well as Christmas.

4. Does the weather ever affect what you do?

— Yes, it surly does to me. On both extremely hot and cold weather, I can't enjoy doing outdoor leisure activities as much as I can if the weather is mild. Occasionally, I have to cancel some dates with my friends if it accidently rains or snows heavily.

Part 2 (3 to 4 minutes)

Topic 4

Describe something you do that is good for your health.

You should say:

what you do

when you began to do it

how often you do it

and explain why you think this is important for your health.

Eating breakfasts used to be the last thing on my morning to-do list, or worse, it was never on my list at all. This was unhealthy. Now I eat breakfasts and I eat good breakfasts, each and every morning—a breakfast which is with top-quality whole wheat. It is more filling, more satisfying, and stays with me longer. So I won't be snacking on un-needed calories after such a healthy breakfast. I started to do this last summer. Since then, the healthy breakfast foods has refueled my body and provided me the foundation for each and every energetic day — a day brimming with health and vigor. It jump-starts my day and may even benefit my overall health. So I think eating breakfasts is important for my health.

wrap-up questions:

- **Would you recommend that to your friends?**

  — Yes, I'd like to tell my friends not to skip this meal — it may be more important than you think.

Part 3 (4 to 5 minutes)

Topic 5 A healthy lifestyle

1. What are some of the things that people do that are harmful to their health?

— Some of the things that people do that are harmful to their health are smoking, drinking too much alcohol, habitually not eating breakfasts, eating too much junk foods, sitting in front of a TV/a computer for too long, having insufficient sleep, and so on and so forth.

2. What do you think are the differences between healthy food and "junk food"?

— Basically speaking, healthy food is fresh and unprocessed whereas in contrast junk food is unfresh and processed. Other distinctive differences between healthy food and junk food are about the shelf life. Comparatively speaking, healthy food has a shorter shelf life while, for junk food, it is the other way round.

3. What things do you think people in China need to do (or need to change) in order to improve their health?

— I think, firstly, people in China need to slightly change their traditional way of diet, that is, drinking more milk and fruit juice at breakfasts instead of having porridge or soy bean milk only which are conventional but not being able to provide sufficient amount of calcium and vitamins needed on a daily basis. Secondly, compared with the pork which is the main meat in a typical Chinese meal, white meat such as chicken and fish are healthier and that Chinese people should eat more of these.

4. More and more people in today's society are overweight. Why do you think this is happening?

— I think there are a couple of reasons contributing to this issue. Firstly, with the fast tempo of life in modern society, many people eat fast food that involves eating lots of junk food which usually contains too much fat and sugar. People put on weight easily with eating that kind of food regularly. Secondly, modern technology has freed people from manual work and enables people to live a comfortable and convenient life. For example, people take a bus or a subway or a taxi or drive their private car to zip around the city rather than walking on foot or riding a bicycle. Yes, it's comfortable and convenient if traveling by modern transportation, yet in the meantime, it has deprived the opportunity of doing some physical exercise. Lack of exercise is another major contributing factor to the reason of why many people are overweight today.

Topic 6 People's health

1. Do you think the media can play a role in educating people about health? (How?)

— Yes, I think the media can guide people and provide information on issues relating to health. Actually, there have already been lots of material, articles, video which are available on various type of media such as newspapers, magazines, the Internet as well as TV. What the media does is that they invite professionals such as doctors, dietitians to contribute their knowledge through the media to the public on health issues.

2. Do you think doctors have a responsibility to give people advice about how to have a healthy lifestyle?

— Yes, I think doctors should tell people how to have a healthy lifestyle. This is because most diseases are caused by bad or unhealthy lifestyles. Doctors are professionals and know best on health care. So with doctors' advice on a healthy lifestyle, people can stay away from certain diseases.

3. Do you think employers have a responsibility to ensure that their employees have a safe and healthy work environment?

— Yes, it's true that employers should make sure that their employees work in a safe and healthy environment. For one reason, it's undoubted that no one wants to work in a dangerous and unhealthy work environment. Who wants to pay their lives simply for an average salary as much as several thousands RMB ? For another reason, employees' working generates profits through which employers develop their business and become prosperous. During the process, employees are only paid with a very small proportion of profits, and along the way, they should be guaranteed with a safe and healthy work environment.

4. Do you think it's a good idea for employers to encourage their employees to live a healthy life? How can employers do that?

— Yes, it is. On one hand, employees can be encouraged by the care that their employers give to them. Thus, they may work harder and contribute more to their employers. On the other hand, employees do gain benefits if their employers focus on the importance of living a healthy life for the employees. Because this focus gives the employers some initiatives to take actions on providing employees with better health care activities. For example, employees can be given free annual physical examinations, or holidays with salary, and so on and so forth.

三、深度透析

Computer & Internet

1. Do you use computers very much/ do you often use the internet?

参考 Do you often write letters? 的答案。

2. What was your impression (or feeling) when you used a computer for the first time?

周计划提示

可用于描写此时情感的词汇有：

fabulous 美妙；fine 美好；good 好；great 非常好；marvelous 奇妙；sensational 极好的；splendid 精彩；superb 雄伟；terrific（美语）妙极，非常好；wonderful 美妙

3. What do you do on the Internet (computer)?

周计划提示

词汇储备：e-mailing, chatting, e-shopping, e-business, watching movies, listening to music, downloading files, searching for information, stock exchange, BBS, blog…

4. What do you think are the benefits of using a computer (the Internet)?

可用于回答电脑和互联网的优点的内容很多，比如从个人角度可以说：学习、工作、生活；从国家角度可以说政治、经济、文化等方面。

从个人角度

- 学习：资源丰富（resources），远程学习（distance education）
- 工作：节省成本（cost），效率提高（efficiency），开拓国外市场（market share）
- 生活：方便（convenient），如：在线购物（online shopping），娱乐性强（entertainment）

从国家角度

- 政治：促进民主（democracy），国际合作（international cooperation）
- 经济：国际贸易发展（international trade），规模经济（mass economy），信息传播快（spread of information）
- 文化：跨文化交际更方便（cross culture communication）

回答可用一般到具体的答题思路，所以本题可作如下回答：

— Well, using a computer and the Internet can benefit both individuals and countries. For individuals, Internet and computers make their work, study and life easier and convenient. For example, in their study, they can share information internationally, which is impossible with libraries only. For countries, Internet and computers made many things impossible possible. For example, the Internet can provide the latest information about economy development all over the world, so it is easier for a country to develop its own economy accordingly.

周计划提示

“讨论优缺点”+“Yes/No”问题回答思路

Computer & Internet

1. Is there anything that's not so good about computers (the Internet)?

凡事皆有好坏。同时讨论优缺点是雅思口语考试非常常见的问题方式。电脑和互联网同样也有缺点，如：电脑辐射 (radiation)，网络安全隐患 (security concern: such as hacker, crime)，色情暴力对轻少年的影响 (violence and porn) 等。

回答的时候，先肯定再谈缺点，如：

— The Internet (computers) benefits human kind a lot, but it also gets disadvantages as well. For example, computer radiation is very harmful to our health, and Internet is often out of control, it is easy for children to get access to some harmful information such as violence and porn, which is very bad to their health.

2．Do you play computer games?

这是一个 yes/no 问题。在回答 yes/no 问题的时候，考生经常犯的错误有：迂回回答、重复问题和措辞不当。

（1）不直接面对，而是迂回回答

比如："Do you often use Internet?" — "I seldom use Internet because I am very busy." 这样答是不妥当的，对于 yes/no 问题，首先要给出肯定或否定的回答，再延伸解释。

稍作修改，可以说：

"No, I don't. I seldom use the Internet because I'm so busy with my work."

"Not really because I'm so busy with my work."

（2）重复问题中的措辞

如："Do you like playing computer games?" "Yes, I like it." 或者是 "No, I don't like it"。这样的答案连 5 分都很难得到。英语本族语使用者在回答问题时不重复实意动词 (like)，也不会重复问句中的名词或名词性词组（playing computer games）。只有当回答者想强调自己的感受时才会重复。如："Yes, I **do** like it but, at the moment, I don't have much time to play it." **do** 在此表强调。

通常，这么回答会更好："Yes, I do but, at the moment, I don't have much time to play it."

（3）选词不当

① "Maybe"

这是中国学员常用的答案，主要是受汉语的影响。西方人更希望有一个更确切的答案，而 maybe 比较含混，几乎等于没回答。

② "I don't know."（永远也不要以此句来完结你的答题）

遇到答不上的问题可以说：For example: "Do you think the internet is a good educational recourse?" — "I'm afraid I can't give you an opinion on that because my parents rarely let me go onto the internet. You know, I'm only 17 years old." 或 "I'm not too clear about that because ... " 或 "I don't know much about that because ... "

另外，在不知道答案时也可以谈出你的想法。如："Do you think internet will take the place of paper work?" — "Well, I'm not sure but I imagine that, yes, it seems that computer can do almost everything now."

③ "Of course."（使用过于泛滥）

这个答案要谨慎使用，往往会有一些感情色彩，似乎在说"这还用问吗"。

在面对 yes/no 问题的时候，最好就是直接回答为：

如：

- Are you going to watch football match tonight? — Yes, I am.
- Do you like sports? — Yes, I do.
- Do you live with your parents? — Yes, I do.
- Have you been abroad? — No, I haven't.
- Can you speak other languages? — No, I can't. /Yes, I can.
- Would you say your hometown is a good place to live? — Yes, I would.

- Will you go to that place again? — No, I won't.

或者是在原有基础上添加一些副词。如：really，certainly，definitely，probably，possibly，usually，often，frequently，sometimes，never 等。

- Do you like singing? — Yes, I really do!
- Would you like to be a leader? — Yes, I certainly would.
- Have you ever been to another country? — No, I never have.
- Did you get the book? — Yes, I eventually did.
- Do you check your email every day? — Yes, I usually do.
- Did you get the job? — Unfortunately, no, I didn't.

还可以用一个单词或短语来回答。如：

- "Absolutely!" ("Absolutely not!")
- "Certainly!" ("Certainly not!")
- "Definitely!" ("Definitely not!")
- "Of course!" ("Of course not!")
- "Totally!"
- "Naturally!"
- "Not really."
- "Not exactly."
- "Not at all!"
- "Not in the least!"
- "Very much so!"
- "I suppose so." ("I suppose not.")
- "I guess so." ("I guess not.")
- "I imagine so."
- "It depends."
- "I'm not really sure but I imagine/guess/suppose so."
- "(Yes.) Frequently!"
- "(Yes.) Often!"
- "(Yes.) Sometimes."
- "(Yes.) Occasionally. "
- "(No.) Never."

Yes/no 问题看似简单，要想答好是很有难度的。这样的问题要想得 5 分是很容易的，但是要想得 7 分就不是那么容易了。因为，往往 yes/no 问题的重心不是在 yes/no 上，而是在后续的解释上。所以，在面对这样的问题时，不管考官是否追问，一定要在回答完 yes/no 之后，近一步解释你为什么会这么认为。

3. Do you think the use of the Internet needs to be controlled?

— Yes, I think so, because the Internet has many disadvantages, and those disadvantages do not lie in the Internet itself, but in how we use it, so certain control would make it more beneficiary.

4. Have you ever bought anything on the Internet?

—No, never. I don't think online shopping is reliable, I have friends who were cheated by online shop owners. They do not tell the truth about the quality of the goods.

5. What do you think are the benefits of "e-learning"?

—Well, I think e-learning is a new trend, which makes the best use of modern technology, by using e-learning, we can share the resource and teaching staff around the world, and we can communicate with more people.

四、拓展问题

Computer & Internet

1. In general, what impact does the Internet have on people's lives?
2. How has the Internet changed your life?
3. Do you think the Internet is a good thing?
4. What are the good and bad points about the Internet?
5. What kinds of people most often use the Internet for work?
6. How can people best make use of the Internet?
7. How can people learn things on the Internet?
8. What sorts of things can (or do) people learn on the Internet?
9. How often do you play computer games?
10. What do you do when your computer has problems?

Rain

1. Does it rain much in China?
2. What do you do on rainy days (or on a rainy day)?
3. What effects can a shortage of rain (a drought) have on people's lives?
4. Does rain ever affect transportation in your hometown? (How?)
5. Do you think the seasons have changed in recent years, compared to the past? (Why? How?)

星期四

第四套真题

一、真题及自测评分表

The Introduction (25 to 30 seconds)

1. Good morning/afternoon. My name is ______ . Can you tell me your full name, please?
2. What shall I call you?
3. Can you tell me where you're from?
4. Can I see your identification, please?

Part 1 (4 to 5 minutes)

Topic 1 Advertisements

1. Do you like advertisements?
2. Have you ever bought anything after seeing (or hearing) an advertisement?
3. What are the differences between advertisements on TV and those in magazines?
4. Do you think advertising plays a very important role in today's world?

Topic 2 Friends

1. Do you have many (close) friends?
2. What do you with your friends?
3. Do you think friendship is important?
4. How do you keep in contact with your friends?

Topic 3 Flowers

1. Do you like flowers?
2. On what occasions do people give flowers to other people?
3. Do you like to have flowers in your home?
4. Have you ever grown flowers at home? (Give details)

Part 2 (3 to 4 minutes)

Topic 4

Describe a success you would like to achieve (in the near future).

You should say:

what it is

how difficult you think it will be

what you should do to prepare for this

And explain why you want to succeed in doing this.

wrap-up questions:

- Can you get some help from others?

Part 3 (4 to 5 minutes)

Topic 5 Success

1. What do you think is a good definition of the word "success"?
2. In (Chinese) society, how is success defined or measured?
3. What kinds of people are most likely to become successful?
4. Can you give me any examples of very successful Chinese people in sports, business or entertainment?

Topic 6 Competition

1. Modern life seems to be quite competitive so why is there competition between university students?
2. What are some of the reasons why people compete against other people?
3. Many people think that being "Number 1" is everything - they think that being Number 2 or Number 3 is not good enough. What do you think of this attitude?
4. For people working in a company, is it more important to be competitive with your work colleagues or be co-operative?

自测评分表

Marking criteria	Band
Fluency and Coherence	
lexical resource	
Grammatical Range and Accuracy	
Pronunciation	
Final band (Average score)	

二、模板答案

The Introduction (25 to 30 seconds)

1. **Good morning/afternoon. My name is Susan. Can you tell me your full name, please?**

   — My name is Wang Ping.

2. **What shall I call you?**

   — Please call me Ping.

3. **Can you tell me where you're from?**

— I'm from Jiangsu.

4. **Can I see your identification, please?**

— Yes, here you are.

Part 1 (4 to 5 minutes)

Topic 1 Advertisements

1. **Do you like advertisements?**

— Yes, I do. They are informative, though I don't deny that they might mislead sometimes. Besides, they are fun in different ways. For example, some advertisements invite celebrity to be the spokeperson of the product. Some use animals to film.

2. **Have you ever bought anything after seeing (or hearing) an advertisement?**

— Yes, I've done that a couple of times. However, my personal experience is that the product was usually not as good as the advertisement described. So, I've learned not to trust everything that the advertisement says.

3. **What are the differences between advertisements on TV and those in magazines?**

— Advertisements on TV are both visual and audio whereas in contrast those in magazines are visual only. Another difference between these two types of media is that, basically speaking, people who watch TV are more than those who read magazines, which means, to some extent, advertisements on TV are more effective than those on magazines.

4. **Do you think advertising plays a very important role in today's world?**

— That's true indeed! Advertising is nonpersonal communication that is designed to communicate in a creative manner, through the use of mass media, the nature of products, services, and ideas. It is used by commercial firms trying to sell products and services; by politicians and political interest groups to sell ideas to persuade voters; by not-for-profit organizations to raise funds, solicit volunteers, or influence the actions of viewers; and by the governments seeking to encourage or discourage particular activities, such as wearing seatbelts, participating in the census, or ceasing to smoke….. You see it is used everywhere, and that's why it plays a very important role in today's world.

Topic 2 Friends

1. **Do you have many (close) friends?**

— Yes, I have many friends, though those I feel close to are few.

2. **What do you with your friends?**

— I usually watch movies and chat with my friends. Sometimes I hang out with them to sing karaoke, or do some window shopping.

3. **Do you think friendship is important?**

— Yes, indeed! There are very few things as precious as having good friends, and friendship is one of the greatest pleasures that people can enjoy. A true friend can really find pleasure in our joy and share sorrow in our grief. When we are in trouble or difficulties, he or she is always at our side to give us help and comfort.

4. How do you keep in contact with your friends?

— There are many ways through which I keep in contact with my friends. To those that I hang out often, I catch them by texting messages or making phone calls through my mobile. To those who live far from me such as friends coming from another country, I usually send emails to them.

Topic 3 Flowers

1. Do you like flowers?

— Yes, I do like flowers. Personally, I see flowers as one of the great creation made by God.

2. On what occasions do people give flowers to other people?

— There are many occasions on which people give flowers to express their feelings and emotions to others. For example, birthdays, weddings, funerals, festivals, anniversaries, and so on and so forth.

3. Do you like to have flowers in your home?

— Yes, I do. I love to have flowers in my home. It not only cheers up my weary heart but also livens the rooms of my house. Flowers in a vase make the dinner table or the living room or even a bedside mini even more homey.

4. Have you ever grown flowers at home? (Give details)

— Yes, I did that when I was a teenager. Actually, my father taught me how to grow flowers in flower pots. I remember one important thing to do when growing flowers in flower pots is that you need to use a big container. Bigger is better. Because a larger pot or container holds moisture longer and also provides more space for the plants' roots. The healthier the root system, the healthier your flowers will be. Also, the container must have a drainage hole in the bottom to allow excess water to escape.

Part 2 (3 to 4 minutes)

Topic 4

> Describe a success you would like to achieve (in the near future).
>
> You should say:
>
> what it is
>
> how difficult you think it will be
>
> what you should do to prepare for this
>
> and explain why you want to succeed in doing this.

In the near future, I would like to start my own animal sanctuary to help those abandoned, injured, mistreated, stray animals living in the urban area. Yes, it is so difficult that it can seem like a dream job. However, it takes a lot of planning and work to have a successful sanctuary. I'm skilled in organization and enjoy working with both people and animals, starting an animal sanctuary may be a dream come true. In order to prepare for this, I need to consider how to fund my sanctuary, purchase land, find a veterinarian who can treat my animals, get a volunteer base to help with animal care and so on. I want to succeed in setting up an animal sanctuary because I found that, living in this human-dominated world, animals are helpless and live a miserable life. You'll understand what I am saying if you watch the video titled "San Hua(the Chinese pinyin)", dated July 5th, 2010 on the websites of www.ku6.com and www.tudou.com. What's more, the movie "Cove" reveals another tip of the iceberg. In addition, I want to succeed in doing this because I want to influence people about helping animals and convey a message that animals do have feelings and emotions just as much as we humans have. Apart from this, they have the cognition as we humans do. Any type of mistreating or killing behaviors are shameful and illegal. Karma-what goes around comes around.

wrap-up questions:

- **Can you get some help from others?**

  — Yes, a friend of mine who is a veterinarian also want to build up an animal shelter. So we have helped each other. Moreover, most of my friends are animal-friendly people, I'm sure they'll help with this.

Part 3 (4 to 5 minutes)

Topic 5 Success

1. What do you think is a good definition of the word "success"?

— Different people define "success" in different ways. Also, an individual may define it differently at different life stages. To me, I am not sure what a good definition of "success" can be, yet I think a general one should be "Get What You Want". Besides, if you are able to donate money, spread happiness, inspire health, propagate love, share knowledge, motivate people, etc. then you are successful.

2. In (Chinese) society, how is success defined or measured?

— In Chinese society, basically speaking, success is defined as having a decent job, living in a big house, having a happy marriage as well as having smart and achieved children.

3. What kinds of people are most likely to become successful?

— In my opinion, people who are not only talented but also hard-working and persistent are most likely to become successful. The singer, Celine Dion; the sports star, David Beckham; the politician, Barack Obama are all good examples for the traits I mentioned the above for being most likely to become successful.

4. Can you give me any examples of very successful Chinese people in sports, business or entertainment?

— Yes! Li Ning, one of the most outstanding athletes in the 20th century, unprecedentedly won six gold medals in men's artistic gymnastics events in the 6th World Cup Competition in 1982. He was named the "Prince of Gymnastics" in the PRC. For business area, I'd like to mention Ma Yun who now serves as chairman and CEO of Alibaba Group. He was named one of the "25 Most Powerful Businesspeople in Asia" by Fortune. As for entertainment, I have to talk about Jackie Chan. He has received worldwide recognition for his acting, having won several awards including an Innovator Award from the American Choreography Awards and a lifetime achievement award from the Taurus World Stunt Awards. He has stars on the Hollywood Walk of Fame and Hong Kong Avenue of Stars.

Topic 6 Competition

1. **Modern life seems to be quite competitive so why is there competition between university students?**

— I personally think that, to university students, part of competing is simply getting experience at competing. If you want to compete in the future and if you wait till you think you're good enough, you won't have any experience in competition yet. So when you do get "good enough" you might not do as well as someone with equal skill that has more experience with competitions. In addition, it definitely is a way of motivation. I get a lot more artwork complete when I have a show to prepare! Just the way it works.

2. **What are some of the reasons why people compete against other people?**

— I would say that most people compete for a combination of reasons which vary according to the individual. Competitors compete because, firstly, they enjoy the inherent activity of competing for the sake of competing (often because of a belief that competitive pressure forces you to bring out your best stuff). Next, they enjoy crushing their enemies, seeing the losers driven before them, and hearing their lamentations. Thirdly, they want the publicity due to winning. This can be because you want to have more teaching gigs or because you simply want to be more popular on the social dance floor.

3. **Many people think that being "Number 1" is everything - they think that being Number 2 or Number 3 is not good enough. What do you think of this attitude?**

— Being NO. 1 means winning, and winning means being happy and getting more confidence. Besides, it interprets that you are one of the best in the area which you are trying to be NO.1 of. I personally think that holding such an attitude can motivate people strongly, thus making more improvements and progress.

4. **For people working in a company, is it more important to be competitive with your work colleagues or be co-operative?**

— As people working in a company work together mainly for the development of the company instead of the development of any individual, the development of any individual ranks the second important in the circumstance, so it's undeniable that being co-operative means more than being competitive which may lead to self-accomplishment only, but not the prosperity of the company. It is the quality of being flexible, supportive, and be willing to compromise which can contribute to the success of the company.

三、深度透析

Flowers

每当被问到"what is your favorite flower?"时，很多考生会毫不犹豫地说："Rose."其实不是说每个考生都喜欢玫瑰，而是充分体现了考生在这个话题上的词汇非常有限。因此有必要掌握一些常见的花名。

carnation	麝香石竹（康乃馨）
chrysanthemum	菊花
daisy	雏菊
gardenia	栀子
forget-me-not	勿忘草
sensitive plant	含羞草
tulip	郁金香
jasmine	茉莉
lilac	丁香
lily	百合
morning glory	牵牛（喇叭花）
narcissus	水仙花
orchid	兰花
peony	牡丹,芍药
rose	玫瑰,月季

除了花的种类外，最为常见的就是花语了，也就是什么花是具备特殊含义的。考生有必要在考前对词汇和文化都做些储备。

adoration（爱慕，崇拜）	——sunflower 向日葵
amiability（友善）	——jasmine 茉莉花
bashfulness（害羞）	——peony 牡丹花
caring（关心）	——yellow rose 黄玫瑰
captive（被你迷住了）	——peach blossoms 桃花
egotism/Conceit（自负，自恋）	——narcissus 水仙花
confidence（自信）	——lilac 丁香花
congratulations（祝贺）	——yellow and red roses 黄玫瑰和红玫瑰

另外，考生需要始终记得雅思是考核语言水平的，不是考核内容的。因此，内容不准确没有关系。其实，考生不管碰到什么关于文化的考题，都可以说："I am not sure, but in my hometown…"，以此开头，无论后面说什么，都是可以的，因为，毕竟中国这么大，文化多样性是全世界认同的。总之，不要因为自己不知道某个文化影响到自己的考试。

四、拓展问题

Neighbors

1. What do you think of your neighbours?

2. How often do you talk to your neighbours?
3. What sorts of problems can arise between neighbours?
4. In what ways can neighbours help each other?

Visitors

1. Do you often invite friends to visit your home?
2. Do you like visitors coming to your home?
3. Do you invite guests to your home during these festivals?
4. When someone visits you, how do you usually show hospitality (or entertain them)?
5. When (you know) people are going to visit you, what preparations do you make?
6. Do you like to visit other people (at their homes)?
7. On what occasions do you visit other people?

Colours

1. What's your favorite color?
2. Do you usually wear clothes in your favourite colour?
3. Are there any colours that have a special meaning in your country?
4. What colour would you choose to paint the walls of your own room?

星期五

第五套真题

一、真题及自测评分表

The Introduction (25 to 30 seconds)

1. Good morning/afternoon. My name is________. Can you tell me your full name, please?
2. What shall I call you?
3. Can you tell me where you're from?
4. Can I see your identification, please?

Part 1 (4 to 5 minutes)

Topic 1 Art

1. Do you like drawing / painting? (Why / Why not?)
2. Do you think children should have art classes in school?
3. Do you think art is necessary (or important) in society?
4. Why do you think people like to put paintings (or other artwork) on the walls of their homes?

Topic 2 Plans and goals

1. Please summarize your plans for the near future.
2. When do you plan to start that?
3. How do you intend to achieve that?
4. Do you plan to spend many years overseas?

Topic 3 Time

1. Do you (usually) wear a watch? (Why?)
2. Have you ever been late for anything?
3. When does time seem to move fast and when does it seem to move slowly?
4. If you could go back in time, what would you do differently?

Part 2 (3 to 4 minutes)

Topic 4

Describe an important letter that you received.

You should say: who wrote it when you received it what the letter was about and explain why it was important.

Possible follow-up questions:

1. Do you still have this letter?
2. Do you often write letters to your family and relatives?

Part 3 (4 to 5 minutes)

Topic 5 Handwritten letters

1. When do people usually write letters by hand?
2. What can we learn from looking at handwritten letters that are hundreds of years old?
3. Is the handwriting of children today as good as it was many years ago?
4. Can people develop friendships by writing to each other?

Topic 6 Letters in the business world

1. Are letters important when doing business? (Why?)
2. What skills are needed to write good business letters?
3. Compare the strengths and weaknesses of letters with those of phone calls when doing business.
4. What are the differences between business letters and personal letters?

自测评分表

Marking criteria	Band
Fluency and Coherence	
Lexical resource	
Grammatical Range and Accuracy	
Pronunciation	
Final band (Average score)	

二、模板答案

The Introduction (25 to 30 seconds)

1. **Good morning/afternoon. My name is Joey. Can you tell me your full name, please?**

   — I'm Tian Hua.

2. **What shall I call you?**

   — Please call me Huahua.

3. **Can you tell me where you're from?**

— I'm from Guangdong.

4. **Can I see your identification, please?**

— Yes, please.

Part 1 (4 to 5 minutes)

Topic 1 Art

1. **Do you like drawing / painting? (Why / Why not?)**

— Yes, I do even though I don't draw/paint well. I like drawing because it's fun and relaxing. It gives you space to be imaginative and creative.

2. **Do you think children should have art classes in school?**

— Yes, I would say it's better to have it than not. In this case, children are able to access to an all-round development, which enhances the possibility of finding their talents and potentials.

3. **Do you think art is necessary (or important) in society?**

— Yes, I think art is necessary, or to some extent, important in society. Art can be a media through which human emotions and thoughts are displayed by the artists and then influence the viewers, or the public with the empathy aroused by the artworks. Good art works can bring positive impacts onto the society and fuel human civilization.

4. **Why do you think people like to put paintings (or other artwork) on the walls of their homes?**

— Some paintings (or other artwork)are made to be decorative. They can beautify rooms in the houses, and cheer up people.

Topic 2 Plans and goals

1. **Please summarize your plans for the near future.**

— I plan to gain a degree in the next couple of years. After that, I'm going to set up my own company.

2. **When do you plan to start that?**

— I plan to start applying for foreign universities as soon as I get the IELTS examination result.

3. **How do you intend to achieve that?**

— As for the degree, all I need to do is study hard. With regards to setting up my own company, I need to accumulate capital and build up a good team.

4. **Do you plan to spend many years overseas?**

— No, I don't. I'm in my prime, and my prime won't last long. I plan to come back to China to start up my company as soon as I obtain the degree overseas.

Topic 3 Time

1. **Do you (usually) wear a watch? (Why?)**

— Usually, I don't wear a watch. I believe, to most people, mobile phones have become the replacement of watches to indicate the time to people.

2. **Have you ever been late for anything?**

— Oh, yeah. The traffic in my city is awful. Even though I always have made sure that I set off earlier than my scheduled time for activities, I still can't manage it sometimes.

3. **When does time seem to move fast and when does it seem to move slowly?**

— When doing something that enables us to feel relaxed and enjoyable, time seems to move fast, and when doing something which needs patience, then time seems to move slowly.

4. **If you could go back in time, what would you do differently?**

— If I could go back in time, I would pay attention to time management at study, work as well as life, which can result in the improvement of efficiency. Furthermore, I would learn to value and appreciate more. I mean value and appreciate the people I know and the things I have.

Part 2 (3 to 4 minutes)

Topic 4

Describe an important letter that you received. You should say: who wrote it when you received it what the letter was about and explain why it was important.

One of the important letters that I received was written by my elder sister. It was back to my college years during which my sister and I wrote to each other once a week. I remember the very first letter she wrote to me. It inspired me greatly. The letter was about how to spend the college years in a meaningful and productive way. 4 points in the letter included: Firstly, desire knowledge and read as many books as possible. Secondly, make as many friends as possible and follow those who are excellent. Thirdly, fall in love if Mr. Right ever shows up. Last, prepare and get ready for working life after graduation. It was an important letter to me as it shed light on my campus life. I learned what were the valuable tasks to achieve during the four-year college education. With the guidance of the letter from my sister, I obtained my degree with honors; I read lots of good books which enlarged my scope of knowledge; I made many friends and a few really close ones; I was both physically and mentally ready for jobs after graduation. All in all, I attributed these achievements of my college years to that letter my elder sister wrote to me. Without it, I would probably have spent my college years like a ship sailing in the ocean without a compass.

Possible follow-up questions:

1. **Do you still have this letter?**

— Yes, I do. I still keep it in my drawer.

2. **Do you often write letters to your family and relatives?**

— Well, I used to. Now, I don't. Instead, I keep in touch with my family and relatives by making phone calls.

Part 3 (4 to 5 minutes)

Topic 5 Handwritten letters

1. When do people usually write letters by hand?

— In an age of computers, I think people may write letters by hand when the other means of communication are not available such as emailing, sending a fax, making phone calls, texting mobile messages and so on. Another situation in which people usually write letters is when people hope to express their genuineness and sincerity through their handwriting.

2. What can we learn from looking at handwritten letters that are hundreds of years old?

— We can learn with what materials the ancestors were using to write such as stones, knives, chisels, ink, brush, or whatever. Also, as most of handwritten letters our ancestors used were hieroglyph, so we can collect some information about the society in which our ancestors lived by researching the look/structure of these handwritten letters.

3. Is the handwriting of children today as good as it was many years ago?

— Generally speaking, with the advent of computers, most of the children's handwriting today are not as good as it was many years ago. Children today simply don't have that much necessity to practice their handwriting unless they are interested in practicing in an artistic way, that is, calligraphy.

4. Can people develop friendships by writing to each other?

— Yes, that's why some people have a pen pal. They frequently write friendly correspondence to each other, during which they exchange information about their study, work and lives, and thus friendships are developed and blossomed.

Topic 6 Letters in the business world

1. Are letters important when doing business? (Why?)

— They are important because business letter has a materialistic purpose but effective business letter can also strengthen the bond between two organizations or the dealer and the customer. Another point is that business letters are used for many purposes such as to make inquiries, send replies, place orders or bank correspondences etc. The main and basic function of the business letter is not only to convey your message to the person who receives the letter but also to influence the reader.

2. What skills are needed to write good business letters?

— Well, I think there are a couple of skills for writing good business letters: Firstly, the language of a business letter should be simple, which means it shouldn't contain difficult words, phrases, or technical jargon. Secondly, avoid use of dull and uninteresting language. Next, sincerity of purpose is important not only for human relations but also for business dealings. Then, avoid self-centered focusing on your own concerns and your business and focus on the recipient's needs, interests, or purposes. Last but not the least, tune your sentences to the taste of the prospective buyer.

3. Compare the strengths and weaknesses of letters with those of phone calls when doing business.

— The strengths of letters when doing business are that the sender can take time to think and organize on things which are going to be mentioned in the letters, and with the reply from the recipient, again, the sender can take time to study the wording of the recipient so as to work out an appropriate reply. While in contrast the strengths of phone calls are that it's prompt, so the business partners can feel that they are closely connected, which may enhance the concentrations on the dealings. With regard to the weaknesses of letters when doing business, I would say that it takes time, and sometimes misunderstandings may occur due to its failing to catch up with the progress/change of the situations. On the contrary, the weakness of phone calls are that it's prompt, and the business partners don't have much time to consider the points which they may feel regretful later mentioned in their conversations on the phone.

4. What are the differences between business letters and personal letters?

— The language used in business letters are more formal whereas in contrast the one used in personal letters are more casual. In addition, generally speaking, the recipients of business letters can be a person or a department, or a company. However, the recipients of personal letters are usually just one individual person, or a couple of people of one family.

三、深度透析

Art

1. Do you like drawing / painting? (Why / Why not?)
2. Do you think children should have art classes in school?
3. Do you think art is necessary (or important) in society?
4. Why do you think people like to put paintings (or other artwork) on the walls of their homes?

对于这四个问题，可以准备同样一个答案，以不变应万变。事实上，这些题都是考核艺术的重要性。

— Well, I think art is essential for me/ children/ society/ my family, because being able to appreciate art works can make one's life more enjoyable, and can help one to make more friends.

Goals, plans, ambitions

很多考生走进考场的时候，并没有明确的人生目标。在碰到这个考题的时候显得非常狼狈。考生要永远记得将考试和自己的实际生活分离。如果真要突然问起你的人生理想，这是一下很难说出来的。因为，这是个非常严肃的问题。但是，毕竟只是口语考试，不需要你特别负责任地回答这个问题，那么就可以随意说了，甚至可以吹牛，哪怕是不可能实现的人生目标，只要能自圆其说，说什么都可以。

Time

现代青年很多已经不带手表了，因为有太多的电子产品具备手表的功能。但人们对时间的感觉、概念和文化态度还依然存在。

Have you ever been late for anything?

面对这个题目，可能很多考生都会说 no。但实际上，对待这样的问题，如果说 yes，将有更多的话可以说，可以更容易保证考试口语的流畅性。

Describe an important letter

也许你很少或者从来没有接到过书信，但是 email 总是很经常的事。所以，不必拘泥，可以拿 email 来替换 letter。但作为一个即将出国的学生，重要信件是很容易想到的，比如：an offer from your ideal university, an friend in another country write to tell you that he/she has rent a flat for you, etc. 这些都是很容易结合考雅思、出国学习和生活等来说的，因此，很容易措辞。

四、拓展问题

Music

1. Do you often listen to music?
2. What's your favourite type of music?
3. What role does music play in the cultural life of people (or of society)?
4. How does music affect (or influence) people?
5. What are some differences between the music you listened to as a child and the music you listen to now?
6. Do you play any musical instruments?
7. Do you think it's important to learn to play a musical instrument?
8. What musical instrument would you like to learn (if you had the time or the chance to learn one)?
9. What advantages do you think there are for a child to learn (to play) a musical instrument (to study music)?
10. Do you think school should teach children how to play a musical instrument?

Daily Routine

1. What do you do in a typical day (at work or at school/university)?
2. What time do you usually get up?
3. What's your favourite time of (or part of) the day?
4. What's your favourite day of the week?
5. What changes would you like to make to your daily routine (or to your life) in the future?

Art Galleries and Museums

1. Are there any museums or art galleries in your hometown?
2. Do you like visiting museums and art galleries?
3. Do people in China like visiting museums and art galleries?
4. What are the benefits (for people/for children) of visiting museums and art galleries?

Photography

1. Do you like to take photographs? (Why?)
2. Do you prefer to take photos yourself or to have other people take photos? (Why?)
3. In what situations do you take photographs?
4. Do you prefer to take pictures of people or of scenery?
5. How do you keep your photos?
6. Do you prefer to send postcards to people or to send photos that you took yourself? (Why?)
7. What is the value of taking photographs?
8. Do you think being a photographer would be a good job? (Why?/Why not?)
9. Why don't some people like having their photo taken?
10. What factors make a good photograph?

Languages

1. What foreign languages have you studied (or learned)?
2. Why did you choose to study that language?
3. What language would you like to learn (if you had the opportunity)? (Why?)

星期六

第六套真题

一、真题及自测评分表

The Introduction (25 to 30 seconds)

1. Good morning/afternoon. My name is________. Can you tell me your full name, please?
2. What shall I call you?
3. Can you tell me where you're from?
4. Can I see your identification, please?

Part 1 (4 to 5 minutes)

Topic 1 Birthdays

1. Which birthdays are especially important in China (in Chinese culture)?
2. How do people in China celebrate birthdays?
3. What did you do on your last birthday?
4. Do you think it's important for people to celebrate birthdays?

Topic 2 Birds

1. How do you feel about birds?
2. Do any birds have any particular significance in China?
3. Do you think birds should be protected? (Why? / Why not? How can they be protected?)
4. Do Chinese people like raising (keeping) pet birds?

Topic 3 Holidays

1. What do you usually (like to) do in your holidays?
2. Do you think it's important for people to have holidays?
3. Do you think people in China need more holidays (vacation time)?
4. Do you think it's reasonable for an employer to ask his or her employees to work in their free time?

Part 2 (3 to 4 minutes)

Topic 4

Describe a TV program that you watched but didn't like.

You should say: what program it was when you saw it what it was about and explain why you didn't like it.

Possible follow-up questions:

- Is that program (that you just talked about) very popular in China?

Part 3 (4 to 5 minutes)

Topic 5 Television tastes

1. In general, what types of TV programs are most popular in China?
2. What do you think are the features (characteristics) of a good quality TV program?
3. Do you think there should be more educational TV programs?
4. Do you think people should have to pay money to watch television?

Topic 6 TV stars

1. Do you think TV celebrities are good role models for children?
2. In your opinion, what qualities does someone need to have to become a TV celebrity?
3. Many TV stars have an income that is very high. Do you think this is reasonable?
4. Do you think that TV celebrities have any responsibilities towards society?

自测评分表

Marking criteria	Band
Fluency and Coherence	
Lexical Resource	
Grammatical Range and Accuracy	
Pronunciation	
Final band (Average Score)	

二、模板答案

The Introduction (25 to 30 seconds)

1. Good morning/afternoon. My name is Martin. Can you tell me your full name, please?

— I'm Zhang Hong.

2. What shall I call you?

— Please call me Hong.

3. Can you tell me where you're from?

— I'm from Liaoning.

4. Can I see your identification, please?

— Yes, here you are.

Part 1 (4 to 5 minutes)

Topic 1 Birthdays

1. Which birthdays are especially important in China (in Chinese culture)?

— The 1st, the 18th and the 60th birthday are especially important in Chinese culture. Usually, people invite their relatives and friends to dinners, or banquets to celebrate these special days in their life.

2. How do people in China celebrate birthdays?

— Traditionally, people eat noodles on their birthdays. The long thread of noodles stands for longevity. In the modern time, people celebrate birthdays by singing "Happy Birthday to You", making wishes, blowing out candles, eating birthday cakes. It is pretty much like the way people celebrate birthdays in the West.

3. What did you do on your last birthday?

— Well, I called my mother to say "Thank You!" to her for giving me life and raising me up. In addition, I bought her a bunch of carnations and a nice brooch. This is a ritual of mine on my birthdays, that is, I please my mother by saying sweet words and buying her nice stuff.

4. Do you think it's important for people to celebrate birthdays?

— Yes. Birthdays, according to the custom, are usually celebrated with family members and friends, which can enhance the kinship and friendship.

— No. To some individuals, birthdays means nothing special than being a year older. What's more, it always comes back a year later. So it's not that important to celebrate, or at least one doesn't have to celebrate each birthday in one's life.

Topic 2 Birds

1. How do you feel about birds?

— Birds are lovely. That's why many people love to raise them as pets. However, the disappointing thing is that they are usually caged once they become pets. This is no good to them.

2. Do any birds have any particular significance in China?

— Yes. In China, traditionally, cranes refers to longevity. Mandarin ducks stands for a happy couple. Also, eagles mean bravery.

3. Do you think birds should be protected? (Why? / Why not? How can they be protected?)

— Yes, I think birds should be protected so as to keep its population at a good level. Many birds eat pests living on the trees as well as crops. They are the guardians. They can help maintain the health of a natural ecosystem.That's why they should be protected. There are many things we can do to protect the birds. One of the best things we can do to protect them around our home is to keep our cats indoors. Millions of birds of different species are killed by domestic cats each year, according to scientific studies. Even birds that survive cat attacks often die from an infection brought on by the cat's claws or teeth.

Keeping our cats indoors will help protect baby birds, and it will also keep our cats safe from cars, attacks by other animals, diseases, and parasites.

4. Do Chinese people like raising (keeping) pet birds?

— Yes. Lots of Chinese people, especially old men, love to raise pet birds. They have a true dedication to taking care of their lives. To those birds' owners, they are more than a bird in a cage. They are a companion for life.

Topic 3 Holidays

1. What do you usually (like to) do in your holidays?

— I usually do some indoor activities such as reading, listening to music, watching movies and so on.

2. Do you think it's important for people to have holidays?

— It surely is. People are not machines, so we need to take days off to have some rest and relaxation so as to get refreshed, which enables us to work and study efficiently again.

3. Do you think people in China need more holidays (vacation time)?

— I think most people in China would agree to have more holidays. Currently, people in China have gained more holiday time than people living in the 1980s and before that. However, comparing to the West, most Chinese people still have less amount of time to smell the flowers and have some quality time.

4. Do you think it's reasonable for an employer to ask his or her employees to work in their free time?

— Well, I guess when an employer has to ask his or her employees to work in their free time, then he or she should at least pay the employees. It'll be nice if the pay is doubled. In this case, it can be reasonable.

Part 2 (3 to 4 minutes)

Topic 4

Describe a TV program that you watched but didn't like.

You should say:

what program it was

when you saw it

what it was about

and explain why you didn't like it.

I watched a TV program called "World Wrestling" about three or four years ago. Yes, from its name, the show was about wrestling, however, lots of violence were involved. I bet you'll feel stunned if you watch it as the wrestlers were trying their best to kill each other instead of doing the normal wrestling as a sport. It's just awfully horrible. I didn't like it because extensive viewing of television violence by people causes greater aggressiveness. Sometimes, watching a single violent program can increase aggressiveness. Young people, especially children, who view shows in which violence is very realistic, frequently repeated or left unpunished, are more likely to imitate what they see. Also, the impact of TV violence may be immediately evident in a child's behavior or may surface years later, and young people can even be affected when the family atmosphere shows tendency towards violence. However, this does not mean that violence on television is the only source for aggressive or violent behavior, but it is a significant contributor.

Possible follow-up questions:

- **Is that program (that you just talked about) very popular in China?**

  — No, it isn't. I came across it when I was doing shopping in a supermarket.

Part 3 (4 to 5 minutes)

Topic 5 Television tastes

1. In general, what types of TV programs are most popular in China?

— Generally speaking, TV news, chat shows, variety shows and soaps are most popular in China.

2. What do you think are the features (characteristics) of a good quality TV program?

— Well, TV, as a means of recreation, a good quality TV program, in my mind, should be first of all entertaining, then if they could be informative, instructive, educative, that would be wonderful.

3. Do you think there should be more educational TV programs?

— Sure, TV, as a type of media, it influences the public, which means we need to be careful with what we put on the TV. If we broadcast more educational programs, it definitely generates positive impact to society.

4. Do you think people should have to pay money to watch television?

— Yes, I think people should pay money to watch television. Because it is a type of service just like the Internet, mobile phones, or whatever. We pay money to get access to the Internet, and we pay money to make phone calls.... So we should pay money to watch television.

Topic 6 TV stars

1. Do you think TV celebrities are good role models for children?

— Well, not all TV celebrities are aware of the influence that they may bring to the young people. Those who are careful with what they say and do when being exposed in the public, because they know their admirers—usually young people—love to follow them, are good role models for children.

2. In your opinion, what qualities does someone need to have to become a TV celebrity?

— I believe charisma and agility are the qualities someone need to become a TV celebrity. There are other qualities which are also required such as being articulate, having a good look and so on.

3. Many TV stars have an income that is very high. Do you think this is reasonable?

— Most TV stars are young people, though Larry King is an exception, which means those who work as TV stars contribute their prime to the TV. On this aspect, I think it is reasonable that they have an high income.

4. **Do you think that TV celebrities have any responsibilities towards society?**

— Yes, they do. I would say that they have great responsibilities towards society. On the one hand, they are the role models which means what they say and what they do influence the society. On the other hand, their incomes are higher than the average, some of them actually possess a great fortune. Therefore, they should contribute more to the charity.

三、深度透析

Birthdays

1. **Which birthdays are especially important in China (in Chinese culture)?**

中国特别重视生日。尤其是整生日往往具备特殊含义，比如：周岁； 十岁；20弱冠（男子）；30而立；40不惑；50知命；60花甲；70古稀；100期颐等。答案见P114。

2. **How do people in China celebrate birthdays?**

中国人一般是吃饭，年轻人也效仿西方人开“party”，也还有其他个性化的庆祝方式。

— Well, traditionally, Chinese people would normally celebrate their birthdays by having a big meal. Sometimes, friends and relatives would gather to celebrate the birthday so as to show their respect to the person. But, young people would often have a party.

Birds

Do any birds have any particular significance in China?

周计划提示

乌鸦 crow ——bad luck, or death
喜鹊 magpie ——good luck, happiness
布谷鸟 cuckoo ——season for growing rice
鸽子 pigeon ——peace
孔雀 peacock ——narcissus
鹰 eagle ——braveness
猫头鹰 owl ——evil
天鹅 swan ——dignity

在其他文化中，有些鸟也有特殊含义。

黑背鸟 blackbird ——A message of blessings
鹤 crane ——Independence
乌鸦 crow ——Divine law
鸽子 dove ——Love, Peace
鸭子 duck ——Good Luck;Wealth
白头鹰（美国国鸟）eagle ——Divine Spirit. To see an eagle is to have divinity touch your life
鹅 goose ——Faithfulness, Communication, Travel

鸥 gull ——Adaptability

鹰 hawk ——Messenger. If you see a hawk, look around, there is a message for you in what is also going on around you

母鸡 hen —— Domesticity. Hens also predict the weather; if they gather on a mound and preen their feathers, rain is on the way. Also if it starts to rain watch your hens if the huddle under shelter, the rain will be of short duration, if they go out into it, the rain will last most of the day

翠鸟 kingfisher ——Predicts a magical experience

百灵鸟 lark ——Great happiness

鹊 magpie ——Fortune-teller

猫头鹰 owl ——Wisdom

鹦鹉 parrot ——Mimic

孔雀 peacock ——Pride, Vanity

知更鸟 robin ——Gypsies see robins as a bringer of good luck

雄鸡 rooster ——Pride

麻雀 sparrow ——Good luck for lovers

燕子 swallow ——Good fortune

天鹅 swan ——Grace

火鸡 turkey ——Give away

啄木鸟 woodpecker ——Guardian

Holidays

1. What do you usually (like to) do in your holidays?

2. What did you do in your last holiday?

3. How do people in China spend their holidays?

这三个问题的回答方式可以借鉴“What do you do in your spare time?”的答案。无非就是sports，travel internet，movie，music，TV，reading，eating，shopping，hobby…换汤不换药。考试的时候灵活处理就可以了。

4. How important are holidays to you?

5. Do you think it's important for people to have holidays?

假期的重要性是众所周知的，比如假期可以让长期工作学习的人们得到一定的休息，从而调整状态；为人们提供一些与家人团聚和旅游的机会；为在职人员提供学习的机会和可能性等。有这些想法，基本上这两个题目也就容易了。如：

— Holidays are very important to me (people), because I (people) need some time to relax after a long period of hard working, and I (people) need some time to be with my family or to help to solve some personal problems, what is more, holidays make it possible for me (some people) to get some training for my (their) career.

6. Is there anything you dislike doing during the holidays?

假期是所有人期待的，但假期也有让人烦恼的地方，如：很多人不喜欢走亲访友；放假的时候娱乐的地方人都特别多；很多服务业假期也放假，导致生活不便等。

— I love holidays, but I do hate visiting relatives during holidays, because that takes much of my time, and I often feel annoyed by the crowd wherever I go in the holidays.

7. Do you think it's reasonable for an employer to ask his or her employees to work in their free time?

— Yes, if they give employees choices. I mean if they do not force their employees to work by any means. Many people are willing to work in their free time because of different reasons. So the policy of working in free time is mutually beneficiary, why not give each side an opportunity?

8. (If working) Do you get paid during your holidays?

— Sure, and they should get extra pay for that, because they sacrifice their free time they deserve to contribute to the development of their companies.

Weekends

1. Where do you spend the weekends?
2. Would you say weekends are important to people?
3. How does the average person in China spend his or her weekend?
4. Do you think people should be asked to work on weekends?
5. Should people be paid overtime for working at the weekend?

四、拓展问题

Animals

1. Do you like animals?
2. What's your favourite animal? (Why?)
3. Are people in your country fond of animals?
4. Do you think cities are suitable places for keeping a pet?

Weekends

针对这个话题的所有考题都跟 holiday 的类似。故答案可以基本一致，只要注意灵活地换掉部分关键词就可以了。

1. What do you like to do on weekends?
2. What are you going to (planning to) do next weekend?
3. What do people in China do on the weekends?
4. Which weekend day do you like more, Saturday or Sunday? What do you usually do on that day?
5. Are weekends important to you?
6. Is it important for people to have weekends off?
7. Do you think working people need to rest on weekends?
8. Do you think people should be asked to work on weekends?
9. Do you think people should be paid more money if they work on weekends (or public holidays)?

10．Do children (or young people) today spend their weekends differently to children (or young people) in the past?

区别主要有：时间少了；活动多了；受科技影响大了；课外学习压力增加了等。

本题可采用一般到具体的答题思路。

— Children in modern society spend their weekends very differently with those in the past. For example, in the past children did not have to spend so much time on courses or study, they can enjoy their weekends, but now children have more weekend activities to choose than in the past because of the influence of modern technology.

星期日

第七套真题

一、真题及自测评分表

The Introduction (25 to 30 seconds)

1. Good morning/afternoon. My name is________. Can you tell me your full name, please?
2. What shall I call you?
3. Can you tell me where you're from?
4. Can I see your identification, please?

Part 1 (4 to 5 minutes)

Topic 1 Emails

1. Do you often write (or send) emails?
2. Do you think emails are useful?
3. What kinds of emails do you send and receive? (Business emails?/Personal emails?)
4. Do you think it is a good thing that some companies send out letters/spam emails for the purpose of advertising?

Topic 2 Noise

1. Do you mind noises? (Do any noise bother you?)
2. What types of noises do you come across in your daily life?
3. What are some of the advantages of quiet places?
4. Would you like to work in a noisy place? (Why?/Why not?)

Topic 3 Swimming

1. Do you like swimming?
2. Is swimming very popular in China?
3. Do you think it's important to know how to swim?
4. What do you think are the benefits of swimming (or the benefits of knowing how to swim)?

Part 2 (3 to 4 minutes)

Topic 4

Describe a change you would like to make to your life in the future. You should say:

what change you would like to make when you would like to make this change how easy or difficult you think this change might be and explain why you would like to make this change.

Possible follow-up questions:

- Have you been thinking about making this change for a long time?

Part 3 (4 to 5 minutes)

Topic 5: People's feelings about change

1. In general, what kind of people (or which groups of people) like change?
2. What are some possible negative effects of change?
3. What do young people want to change most when they become adults?
4. Who do you think likes change more, children or adults? Why?

Topic 6: Personal change

1. What are some personal changes that occur only over quite a long time?
2. Do you think it's easy for people to make changes in their lives (or to make changes to themselves)?
3. Why do adults find it harder to change than children?
4. What are some of the typical changes that people experience in their lives?

自测评分表

Marking criteria	Band
Fluency and Coherence	
Lexical Resource	
Grammatical Range and Accuracy	
Pronunciation	
Final Band (Average Score)	

二、模板答案

The Introduction (25 to 30 seconds)

1. **Good morning/afternoon. My name is Susan. Can you tell me your full name, please?**

   — I'm Wang Peng.
2. **What shall I call you?**

   — Please call me Peter.
3. **Can you tell me where you're from?**

   — I'm from Qingdao.
4. **Can I see your identification, please?**

   — Yes, please.

Part 1 (4 to 5 minutes)

Topic 1 Emails

1. Do you often write (or send) emails?

— Yes, I do. I write emails to my friends, classmates, teachers, parents as well as relatives. Through emails, I can keep a constant contact with people I know, and share information with them.

2. Do you think emails are useful?

— Yes, I think emails are very useful. As you may know, lots of people nowadays choose to work at home, the way that help keep them in touch with their boss or colleagues is through emailing. Besides, to those who stay far apart while needing to stay in contact, emails are probably the best way to help out.

3. What kinds of emails do you send and receive? (Business emails?/Personal emails?)

— Mainly, I send and receive personal emails as I'm a full-time student and don't have a job, so I don't get business emails. Besides, I sometimes receive spam emails promoting certain products or service, which is quite bothering. Some of them are even dangerous as they may carry computer viruses.

4. Do you think it is a good thing that some companies send out letters/spam emails for the purpose of advertising?

— Well, from the companies' side, it can be a good thing to do this, and that's why they do it. However, from my personal point of view, I don't think it's good. Based on my personal experience, I've received those kinds of letters and I've never opened up to read them. As soon as I figure out they are spam emails, I delete them right away. I think I'm just one of the thousands of people who deal with them like this.

Topic 2 Noise

1. Do you mind noises? (Do any noise bother you?)

— Yes, very much. Noises from traffic or construction sites bother me a lot. Anyway, I feel irritated at any kind of noise.

2. What types of noises do you come across in your daily life?

— Living in a city like Beijing, I usually hear the noises of traffic, music played aloud to attract more customers at the shops as well as the noise of construction.

3. What are some of the advantages of quiet places?

— While being in a quiet place, it's easier to concentrate, to think logically and rationally. In a word, it's good for my mind work. Also, quiet places enable people to feel relaxed and light-hearted, or whatever type of positive feeling human has.

4. Would you like to work in a noisy place? (Why?/Why not?)

— No. Never! What kind of work I do, I bet I need to focus and think a organized way. A noisy place drives me crazy, and I don't think I can do anything in such a circumstance.

Topic 3 Swimming

1. **Do you like swimming?**

   — Yes, I do. But, honestly speaking, I don't swim well. Among the 4 most common swimming strokes such as freestyle, backstroke, breaststroke and butterfly, I can only manage to do freestyle.

2. **Is swimming very popular in China?**

   — Yes, it is. In most of the cities in China, there are public swimming pools available to the public. Some of them are indoor. Some are outdoor. In summer, the outdoor ones are the most crowded. In winter, some people go swimming in the indoor ones.

3. **Do you think it's important to know how to swim?**

   — Definitely! Swimming is not only an leisure activity for fun but it's also a skill for surviving. For example, in a natural disaster such as flood, or accidently falling into water. If one knows how to swim, there is a good chance for survival.

4. **What do you think are the benefits of swimming (or the benefits of knowing how to swim)?**

   — For one thing, swimming is a type of physical exercise, and it's a good one as when one swims, each and every piece of muscle of his body gets exercised. For another, like what I mentioned earlier, it's a type of skill one can use to either save life of oneself or others.

Part 2 (3 to 4 minutes)

Topic 4

Describe a change you would like to make to your life in the future. You should say: what change you would like to make when you would like to make this change how easy or difficult you think this change might be and explain why you would like to make this change.

A change I would like to make is that spending some quality time so as to enjoy life instead of being a workaholic for the sake of money, power and fame. I would like to make this change because I hold an attitude that we work to live, not live to work. Plus, life is short. So hopefully, when I reach my mid-forties, I could make this change happen in my life. By then, through working hard, I assume I'd be a kind of developed as well as shaped on many aspects of life such as career, family, friends, hobbies and interests, savings, or whatever. These achievements would justify how much I deserve to spend some quality time to enjoy life. For example, cruise on the Caribbean Sea, ski at the resorts of Austria; drink old wines with family and friends; do some reading while lying in bed on a rainy day and so on and so forth. Wow! I just can't wait to make that change happen. Yet in the meantime I firmly believe that in order to spend some quality time in my mid-forties, I have to work diligently and make myself busy as a beaver now in my early twenties. Otherwise, those quality times for my mid-aged years would be just a daydream.

Possible follow-up questions:

- **Have you been thinking about making this change for a long time?**

  — Yes, I have. Also, I think of this change often, especially when I get tired at work.

Part 3 (4 to 5 minutes)

Topic 5 People's feelings about change

1. In general, what kind of people (or which groups of people) like change?

— Young people like change. They don't like old things or to keep things the same for long days.

2. What are some possible negative effects of change?

— Well, change generates a feeling of excitement to us. It refreshes us and arouses our curiosity. In the mean time, we can also feel a kind of lost or confused. A feeling of uncertainty or even insecurity about anything new broght into our life by the change is likely to make us feel stressed, which might result in low efficiency and low productivity.

3. What do young people want to change most when they become adults?

— Personally, I think what they want to change most is the way that people look at them. Before they become adults, they were kids, and that's the way that people looked at them and treated them. When they become adults, they want others to see them as any other adult. They want to be respected as an adult, they want to be listened to, and they want to take responsibility.

4. Who do you think likes change more, children or adults? Why?

— In a general sense, maybe children like change more than adults do. We often see children cry as they get bored with the things they have. Or they can be pleased by anything new to them. They have strong curiosity which drives them to seek new things which change can always bring them.

Topic 6 Personal change

1. What are some personal changes that occur only over quite a long time?

— Generally speaking, getting old, getting a degree, having more savings at the bank, learning to speak a language well, becoming grandparents, getting rid of bad habits(this change may never happens). These personal changes all take time to happen.

2. Do you think it's easy for people to make changes in their lives (or to make changes to themselves)?

— Well, it depends what kind of change. Some changes can happen easily. Some are difficult to achieve, or it may never happen! For example, spending more time on leisure activities rather than on work or study is a very nice change which is easy for people to make it happen. However, if the changes that people want to make it happen are related with personalities, then it's rather difficult, or it takes a long time.

3. Why do adults find it harder to change than children?

— To the adults, growing up is a process of developing during which they learn knowledge, they form their characters, they shape their outlooks. Generally speaking, the whole process takes about 20 years which is actually the time an individual receives his education. If an adult wants to change anything of himself which is the result of 20 years' shaping process, it is of course very difficult. However, children are still in the process of shaping, and shaping can be interpreted as making changes, specifically, to change in a way we aim to be. Therefore, a change is easier to make to a child rather than to an adult.

4. **What are some of the typical changes that people experience in their lives?**

— Commonly speaking, going to school, getting a job, getting married, having children are the typical changes that most people experience in their lives.

三、深度透析

Emails & Letters

1. **Do you often write letters?**

周计划提示

可以用于表示频率的副词有：

always 总是；occasionally 偶尔；often 经常；rarely 很少；frequently 经常；from time to time 有时候；seldom 很少、不常；hardly ever 几乎从不；sometimes 有时候；never 从不

本题回答参考：Frankly speaking, I have never written a real letter, cos I normally use Internet and mobile phone to communicate with people.

2. **When was the last time you wrote an email?**
3. **On what occasions do you write letters / emails?**

— Actually I seldom write letters, the only letter I have written is the time that I wrote to my boy friend for the first time, in which I told him that I loved him, and that was the last letter for him as well.

4. **Which do you prefer to write, emails or letters?**
5. **What are the differences between emails and letters?**
6. **Which do you think is easier to write, a letter or an email?**
7. **Do you prefer to write by hand or write using the computer (or using a keyboard)?**

第 4～7 题是比较书信和电子邮件的区别，二者区别可以从多个方面进行比较，比如：时间、成本、正式程度、功效等。

回答的时候可以用一般到具体的回答思路。如：

— Basically, emails and letters are quite the same, or similar, but they do have differences in cost, efficiency, formality as well as function. For example, emails reach the receivers immediately, while letters need time to be delivered, and letters are paid individually, while emails are almost free except the fee for Internet access.

8. **What are the advantages of emails (compared to letters)?**
9. **Do you think there are any (possible) negative points about emails?**

第 8、9 两个问题考电子邮件的优缺点。答题内容可以借鉴上面的题目。跟书信相比，电子邮件更快捷、更实惠、更便于操作，但是，电子邮件也显得不够正式，而且很容易泄漏邮件内容。

— Emails are developed on letters, therefore, compared to letters, they have many advantages, for example, they are quicker, more economical, and easier to send.

— Although, emails are becoming increasingly popular because of their advantages. They have negative points as well. For example, the safety of emails is often questioned. It is harder to control since they are sent through the I Internet.

相关问题还有：

10. Do you think computers might one day replace handwriting?

11. What sorts of letters (or emails) do you think are the most difficult to write?

— Well, I find that it is always difficult to write a letter or email, but the application letters are the most difficult ones to write, because I have to consider many aspects, such as the tone, the formality, and wording. I have just finished writing an application letter to a university in the UK. I spent days on it. It is really a headache.

12. Which do you think is harder to write, business letters or personal letters?

— Business letters are difficult to write, but comparatively speaking, personal letters may be harder, because more emotions may involve in the letter writing, and sometimes, it is so subtle to control wording. It is easy to have misunderstandings.

13. Do you prefer to receive a phone call or a letter?

14. Which do you prefer, to write a letter, write an email or make a phone call?

书信和电子邮件、电话的比较或者是三者之间的比较，都殊途同归，回答的时候可以互相借鉴。

Sport (and Exercise)

周计划提示

词汇储备

boat race 赛艇	boxing 拳击	cycling 自行车	diving 跳水
Jogging 慢跑	Tai Chi 太极拳	Running 跑步	Bungee jumping 蹦极
baseball 棒球	wrestling 摔交	skiing 滑雪	basketball 篮球
mountaineering 登山	fencing 击剑	football 足球	horizontal bar 单杠
hurdle race 跨栏比赛	Archery 箭术	judo 柔道	parallel bars 双杠
table tennis 乒乓球	surfing 冲浪	softball 垒球	roller skating 滑旱冰
tennis 网球	volleyball 排球	badminton 羽毛球	weightlifting 举重
swimming 游泳	freestyle 自由泳	butterfly 蝶泳	breast stroke swimming 蛙泳
back stroke 仰泳			

1. Do you like (to play/to do) any sports? (What sport?)

2. What kind(s) of physical exercise do you do to keep fit?

3. What kinds of exercise do you think are most suitable for children?

4. In the future, what sports would you like to play (or take part in / or learn)?

这几个题目的答案很容易落入俗套，大部分同学对这些问题的回答都是 football, basketball, table tennis, swimming 和 badminton，让考官觉得非常枯燥、乏味。其实，考官不管你究竟做什么运动，只关注语言质量。这样的答案反映出考生词汇严重不足。所以，在回答这个问题的时候要特别注意个性化。回答取决于你擅长说哪一个体育话题。

如：

— Well, I am crazy about sports, and quite recently I have developed my inertest in weightlifting, because that would help me to develop my muscles, which would eventually make me more attractive to girls.

5. Do you use any equipment for this exercise (or sport)?

6. What sports facilities did you (or do you) have in your high school?

7. Are there any sports facilities near where you live? (for the public to use)

这三个题目的难点在于健身设备的英语表达。但如果特意准备，考试的时候能说出一两个健身器材，如：upright cycle 立式健身车，incline trainer 上斜跑步机，step 负重踏步机，treadmills 踏步机，military press 肩部推举机，weights 哑铃等，就足以震撼考官，当然也能获得考官欣赏。

如：

— Since my aim is to develop muscles, and I have talked with my coach, who suggested me to use military press, which is very helpful. I practice on it for about 20 minutes every day.

8. Do children in China play much sport (or do much exercise)?

— I think children in China play much less sports than they should do; they spend too much time on school work and computers.

9. Do you think it's important to have P.E. classes (or sports classes) at school? (Why?/Why not?)

— Well, I would say, P. E. classes are very essential at school, because children are growing, they need a lot of exercise to develop themselves physically and mentally.

四、拓展问题

Emails & Letters

1. How do you feel when you receive letters or emails?
2. On what occasions do you write letters?
3. What sorts of letters (or emails) do you think are the most difficult to write?
4. Do you usually write letters to people or do you usually use a cell-phone or email?
5. What are the differences between handwritten letters and emails?

Sounds

1. Do you prefer a quiet environment or an environment with some sounds?
2. What natural sound do you like (the most)? (Why?)
3. What sounds do you dislike? (Why?)

4. What sounds remind you of your childhood?
5. How do you feel when you hear your national anthem?

Mobile Phones

1. Do you use a cell phone?
2. What do you use it for?
3. When did you start using a mobile phone?
4. Is there anything you dislike about using cell phones?

Sport

1. Do you like sport?
2. What kind of sport is popular in China?
3. Do you think extreme sport should be banned?
4. What are the benefits of playing sports?

Swimming

1. Can you (or do you) swim?
2. When did you learn to swim?
3. Who taught you to swim?
4. How did you learn to swim?
5. Do you like swimming?
6. Is swimming very popular in China?
7. Have you ever tried to learn to swim?
8. Do you think it's important to know how to swim?
9. What do you think are the benefits of swimming (or the benefits of knowing how to swim)?
10. Do you think swimming should be taught in school?

第三周　7 天强化：

熟悉 7 大雅思口语考试重点

本周学习目标：

本周是雅思口语学习的强化阶段，主要解决雅思口语考试的重点，尤其是第 2 部分问题的解答方案。本周分 7 天，分别学习雅思口语考试的重点话题，即：人物描写，地点描写，物体描写，事件描写，故事描写，活动描写和经历描写。通过深入学习这 7 个考试重点话题，考生将基本掌握雅思口语考试第 2 部分问题的回答思路，并积累最为常见的答题模板和语言素材。

本周学习目录：

星期一	人物描写：A Friend A Child An Old Person Who You Admire A Person Who Has Visited Your Home A Person You Live With
星期二	地点描写：A Historic Site A Place with a Lot of Water A City You Have Visited or Lived in Your Favourite Part of Your Hometown A Place Where You Like to Go Shopping
星期三	物体描写：A Childhood Toy Something You Made by Hand An Old Thing in Your Family A Photograph An Electrical/Electronic Product
星期四	事件描写：A Traditional Event A Family Event A Recent Happy Event A Public Event A Sports Event
星期五	故事描写：The Latest Book You Have Read An Interesting News A Story from TV A Well-known Story from Your Conntry A Story Happened on You or Your Friends
星期六	活动描写：Childhood Game A Leisure Activity A Picnic or Outdoor Meal A Performance A Party
星期日	经历描写：An Occassion When You Were Late A Trip A Science Lesson A Hoppy Childhood Meniory A Success You Have Had

星期一

人物描写

人物描写是雅思口语考试第 2 部分重复次数最多的话题。迄今为止，在第 2 部分出现的人物话题多达数十个。如：

1. Describe a classmate of yours
2. Describe a happy person
3. Describe a colleague
4. Describe your own personality
5. Describe an old person who has influenced you the most
6. Describe a successful person
7. Describe a singer
8. Describe a sportsman
9. Describe a movie star
10. Describe a character in TV or movie
11. Describe a teacher of yours
12. Describe a famous person that you want to spend a day with
13. Describe the oldest person you know
14. Describe a person you visited
15. Describe a child you know
16. Describe a friend
17. Describe a childhood friend
18. Describe an adventurous person
19. Describe a good neighbour (2006.5.13)
20. Describe a character from a childhood story (2006.5.20)
21. Describe someone who spoke a different language (2006.9.2)
22. Describe two people from the same family (2006.9.16)
23. Describe a leader (2006.9.23)
24. Describe a person you live with (2007.1.6)
25. Describe someone who does something well (2007.2.3)
26. Describe an interesting old person (2007.5.12)
27. Describe a person you enjoy talking with (2007.5.19)
28. Describe a person who took care of you in your childhood (2007.6.2)

29. Describe a person who likes to help others (2007.6.2)
30. Describe someone you like to spend time with (2007.6.9)
31. Describe a person you would like to be similar to (2007.9.1)
32. Describe a school friend (2007.9.1)
33. Describe a teenager you know (2008.1.10)
34. Describe a person who has visited your home (2008.1.10)
35. Describe a person who is good at his/her Job (2008.1.10)
36. Describe an old person who you admire (2008.5.10)
37. Describe someone you enjoy spending time with（第二次出现）(2008.8.16)
38. Describe someone who is good at cooking (2008.9.6)
39. Describe your best friend (2008.9.6)
40. Describe a family member (2009.1.10)
41. Describe someone who gave you important help (2009.5.9)
42. Describe an intelligent person (2009.9.5)
43. Describe a family friend (2009.9.5)
44. Describe an old person (2009.11.14)
45. Describe a famous person（第三次出现）(2010.1.9)

虽然人物描写这个话题被反复修改，但无论怎么改，都是换汤不换药，无非还是人物描写。人物描写有比较固定的思路。只要掌握了这个思路，无论碰到什么样的人物描写题都会游刃有余。

一、例题：A Friend

Describe a friend. You should say: how you first met this person how long you have been friends what you do together and explain what you like about this person.

1. 审题、构思

人物描写的思路：

- 外貌特征
- 性格特征
- 举例说明
- 总体评价

2. 素材准备

（1）外貌特征

人的外貌特征主要从以下几个方面去描写：

- 身材
- 体形
- 头发（长短，颜色，发型）
- 面部（脸型、表情、眼睛、鼻子、眉毛、耳朵）
- 肤色
- 衣着

整体描写

beautiful	美丽的
charming	迷人的
sweet	可爱的
handsome	英俊的
peculiar-looking	长相特别的
rough-looking	粗野的
ill-looking	长相丑陋的
good-looking	长得好看的
ugly-looking	长得难看的
funny-looking	长相滑稽的
ordinary-looking	长相一般的
pretty	漂亮的
lovely	可爱的
attractive	有吸引力的

身材

Tall	高的
Short	矮的
of medium height	中等身材
medium height	中等身材
average height	一般身材
below average	低于平均身高
tallish	有些高的
middle-sized	身高中等的
slight	瘦小的
well-built	身材魁梧
1.78 meters	身高1.78米
Lengthy	高（且瘦）
big	高（但不瘦）
leggy	长腿（用于形容女性）

体型

overweight	超过标准体重的

fat	胖的
chubby	圆圆的；胖胖的
round	圆圆的
obese	肥胖
big	大块头
thin	瘦
slim	苗条
slender	苗条的
skinny	非常瘦
skin and bone(s)	皮包骨的瘦
boney	皮包骨的瘦
scrawny	有点惨不忍睹的瘦
lean	瘦（用于有运动习惯的人）
of medium build	中等体型
strong	身体强壮的

脸型

round	圆的
thin	瘦的
long	长的
square	方的

面部特征

freckles	雀斑
pimples	青春痘，脓疱
lines/wrinkles	皱纹
bags under the eyes	眼袋
crow’s feet at the corners of the eyes	眼角的鱼尾纹
scar	伤疤
beauty spots	美人痣
dimples	酒窝

笑容

bright	欢快的
broad	无所顾忌的
charming	可爱的
cunning	狡猾的
faint	不明显的
happy	高兴的
pleasant	令人愉快的

sad	伤心的
sweet	甜蜜的
pleased	满意的
grinning	露齿而笑的
smirking	傻笑的
friendly	友好的
warm	温暖的，热情的
cold	不热情的

眼睛

almond-shaped	杏眼
beadlike	小而亮的眼睛
beautiful	美丽的
big/large	大的
bright	明亮的
bulging	眼珠突出的
close-set	离的很近的
deep-sunken /deep-set	深陷的
sunken	凹陷的
bulging/protruding	凸出的
dewy	水灵灵的
dreamy	梦幻般的
glazed	呆滞的
gentle	柔和的
fishlike	呆板的
hollow/sunken	凹陷的
longsighted/farsighted	远视的
myopic/shortsighted	近视的
round	圆的
sexy	性感的
sharp	锐利的
slanting	斜的
small/tiny	小的
squint	斜视眼的
starry	明亮的
watery	水汪汪的
wide-spaced	分的很开的
swollen	肿胀的
eyelashes	睫毛

eyebrows	眉毛
thick eyebrows/bushy eyebrows	男性的粗浓眉毛
finely arched eyebrows/pencil-thin eyebrows	女性弯弯的柳叶眉

鼻子

long	长的
straight	挺直的
big	大的
small	小的
flat	扁平的
hooked	钩状的
Roman nose	高鼻梁

嘴部

tooth	牙齿
even	整齐的
uneven	不整齐的
chin	下巴
double chin	双下巴
pointed chin and hollow cheeks	尖尖的下巴和凹陷的双颊
lip	嘴唇
thick lips	厚嘴唇
thin lips	薄嘴唇
cherry lips	红嘴唇
forehead	额头
high forehead	额头高
lined forehead	有皱纹

发型

short hair	短发
long hair	长发
straight	直的
curly	卷发（自然卷）
wave	卷发（烫发）
pigtails	辫子
crew cut	平头
bald	秃头的

发色

white-haired	白头发的
jet-black	乌黑的
fair	金色的

blonde	淡黄色的
golden	金黄色的
dyed	染色的
brunette	浅黑色的
mousey	灰褐色的
chestnut	栗色的

皮肤

dark complexioned	肤色黑的
tanned	褐色/古铜色的
a perfection complexion	好皮肤

服饰

smart	潇洒的
scruffy	邋遢的
well-dressed	衣着华丽的
formal	正式的
casual	随便的
conservative	不显眼的
elegant	优雅的
fashionable	时髦的
suave	文雅的
untidy	不整洁的

具体服饰

suit	套装
dress	女装，连衣裙
jeans	牛仔裤

（2）性格特征

warm-hearted	热心肠的
kind-hearted	好心的
bad-tempered	脾气不好的
near-sighted	近视眼的
far-sighted	远视眼的
naughty	淘气的
easy-going	温和宽容的
smart	精明的
wise	明智的
bright	聪明的
diligent	勤奋的
lazy	懒惰的

clever	聪明的
humorous	幽默的
funny	滑稽的
silent	沉默的
talkative	话多的

（3）举例说明

主要描写：stories about the person, events happened on the person.

（4）总体评价

主要描写：why you like this person, why you chose to describe this person, the influence he/she has on you.

周计划提示

人物描写句型储备

I would like to describe a person who…

The reason that I choose to describe him/her is because…

The reason that we are best friends is…

I think the best time we ever had was….

We have many things/friends in common such as….

We first met in middle school.

I enjoy being with him/her and we talk to each other on a daily basis.

描写男性的句子总结：

He was wonderfully good-looking, with his black hair, his clear-cut face, and his blue eyes. He was popular with both men and women.

He was small at first, but he came on quickly. He was a beautiful child, with dark curly hair, and dark-blue eyes which changed gradually to a clear grey.

He is a heavy man, bald, with scarred and brutal face.

He used to be middle-sized, but when he is getting old, he is becoming short.

His eyes are deep-set because he has worked till midnight for a long time.

He was born a hooked nose.

His nose is very big.

He is a middle-aged man who already has double chins and receding hairline.

He easily loses his temper.

描写女性（容貌）的句子总结：

She was young, with a fair, calm face that showed a certain strength.

A girl with long straight hair.

The girls had blond curls.

She is a slim girl.

She is a little overweight.

Her face is getting round.
Her hair is brown and curly.
She is a beautiful girl with fair hair.
He had the most beautiful blue eyes I had ever seen.
She has a double chin.
She is charming when she smiles.
She has a very pleasant smile and she always has a twinkle in her eye.
She always dress very elegant and tidy.
The young woman was tall, with a figure of perfect elegance.
When she smiled, she showed her white even teeth.
There is always a smile of contentment on her face.
She belongs to those who are very difficult to satisfy.
Her appearance fairly took my breath away.

3. 人物描写范文（Describe a friend）

I would like to describe one of my best friends whose name is George. We have been friends for more than twenty years, because we were always in the same class from primary school to university.

外貌特征

Frankly speaking, he is not good looking at all, but he is very popular with both girls and boys.

He is kind of overweight, with a big bald head. He is short-sighted, so he wears a pair of big thick glasses, which makes him look funny, many people burst into laughter when they first see him. However, he doesn't mind it at all, because he is accustomed to it.

性格特征

And he is very extrovert, open-minded and humorous which made him one of the most popular guys in the school.

举例说明

You know, I have never figured out how he got so many jokes and funny stories stored in his mind. He often makes people laugh, so being with him is a very enjoyable thing.

I still remember that when we first entered university, he got himself famous on the very first day, because of his humor.

总体评价

I admire him, and I feel lucky to be his friend, because he helped me a lot and he makes a big difference to my life.

4. 人物描写模版

开场白

I would like to describe ___________ whose name is _______________. We have ____________ for more than twenty years, because ______________ .

外貌特征

Frankly/generally speaking, he/she is very +整体外貌特征描写+具体外貌特征描写（最好能为后面的性格描写埋下伏笔）。

性格特征

and he is very+性格特征（最好与前面的外貌描写想吻合，而且选择的素材应易于用故事来说明，为下面的描写做铺垫）。

举例说明

You know，举一个故事或者事件来说明性格特征，与前面的描写相符。

总体评价

整体评价一下这个人的为人或对你的影响等来结束描述。

二、练习

Describe a child you know.

You should say:

how you know him or her

what he or she likes to do

what kind of person he/she is

and explain how you feel about this child.

1. 范文（Describe a child you know）

I would like to describe a child that I have seen on a TV program. He is called A Bao. I became a fan of his since the first time I saw him.

I would say he deserves his name, which means treasure in Chinese. He is only about 5 years old, but he is very eloquent and humorous, a real treasure for the bored audience.

The first time I saw him, he was being interviewed in a talk show. He was very smartly dressed, but he looked humorous. His head is shaved with only very little hair in the middle of his head, and he was wearing a red waist coat, which made him look very healthy. He always wears a smile on his face, which makes him very lovable and laughable. He makes all the audience burst into laughter constantly.

He is so humorous that every move of his would make the audience laugh. For example, when he finished answering one question of the interviewer, he said: "It's time to clap your hands", of course all the audience gave him a very long applause.

Frankly speaking, I didn't like talk shows, because they are usually very boring. However, I finished watching that interview, and I had been laughing during the program. I think his real humor and honest talking made the interview very precious. I am looking forward to his next talk show.

2. 举一反三

Describe an old person who you admire.

You should say

who this person is

how you know this person (or where you first met him or her)

what kind of person he or she is (or what he or she is like)

and explain why you admire this person.

Describe a person who has visited your home.

You should say:

who the person was

why they visited your home

how you spent the time with this visitor (or how you entertained this visitor)

and explain how you felt about the visit.

Describe a person you live with (or who you spend the most time with).

You should say:

who this person is

what kind of person he or she is

what you usually do (when you are) together

and explain why you (like to) spend time with this person.

3. Related part 3 questions

A Child

1. What do you think about children playing electronic games?
2. Do you think children should spend more time on outdoor activities or more time on indoor activities?
3. How do you think children benefit from playing with toys?
4. Who usually disciples children in Chinese families, the mother or the father?
5. Do you think hitting children is sometimes necessary for discipline? (Why?)
6. What kinds of problems do children have nowadays? How can we resolve these problems?
7. Compare the advantages and disadvantages for children of large families and small families?
8. How do grandparents influence the development of children?

An Old Person Who You Admire

1. Nowadays, what role do old people play in the family?
2. Have attitudes towards old people changed much in recent years?
3. Do you think old people should work?
4. In your country, is there any discrimination against old people if they are applying for a job?
5. What are the benefits of hiring old people for some jobs?
6. Do you think there should be a set age at which people must retire from work?
7. After retirement, how do you think life for old people is different to life for younger people?
8. What do you think are the results on society of having many old people in the community?
9. Who do you think should take care of old people, families or the government?
10. Some old people are very lonely. Can you suggest any way to help them feel less lonely?

A Person Who Has Visited Your Home

1. In your country, when people visit others, do they usually bring anything (as a gift) to give to their host?
2. What sorts of things do you need to pay attention to if you have foreigners visiting your home?
3. And what do you think a foreign guest needs to pay attention to when visiting someone's home in your country?

A Person You Live with

1. In China today, what is the structure of the typical family?
2. In what ways do you think the number of people in a family (a household) affects the family?
3. Do you think China's "One Child Policy" pleases everybody?
4. What do you think are some of the advantages and disadvantages of big families as opposed to small families?
5. What are some of the problems that people can have when they have many children?
6. What are some of the pros and cons of three generations living together?
7. What do you think are some differences between children being brought up by their grandparents and being brought up by their parents?
8. Do you think people should maintain a close relationship with members of their family? (Why?)
9. Some parents are too busy to spend much time with their children. What's your opinion of this situation?
10. What responsibilities do you think young people (and/or children) should have towards their family?
11. Do you think modern technology such as computers and the cell-phones play a positive role in family relationships?
12. In a family, do you think it's important that the man and woman have set (clearly defined) roles to play?
13. Do you think women who have young children should stay at home and take care of the children or should they have the freedom to take a job outside the home, the same as men?
14. To what extent do you think (married) men should do such activities as child-rearing, doing the housework, cooking and shopping for groceries?
15. Do you think it's important for neighbours to help each other?

星期二 地点描写

描写一个地点在雅思口语中的出题频率非常高。常考的话题如下：

1. A Building in Your Hometown	14. A Polluted Place
2. A Building in Your School or University	15. An Ideal Park
3. A Cafe or Restaurant	16. An Historic Site
4. A Garden	17. Your Childhood Home
5. A Hotel	18. Your Childhood Room
6. A Leisure Centre	19. Your Favourite Part of Your Hometown
7. A Library	20. A Restaurant You Like
8. A Modern Building	21. A Small Shop
9. A Place Where People Listen to Music	22. A Tourist Attraction
10. A Place for Swimming	23. An Open-air Market
11. A Place for Shopping	24. Ideal Home
12. A Place with a Lot of Water	25. A City You Have Visited or Lived in
13. A Polluted City	26. Your Work or Study Place
	27. A (Place In A) City You Visited

虽然每个地点不一样，但是描写思路是相同的。下面我们就以一个具体的题目来深入学习地点描写的思路。

一、例题：An Historic Site

Describe an interesting historic site that you have visited.

You should say:

where it was

what you saw at this site

how you first learned about this place

and explain what interested you about that place.

为了保证考试的时候答案足够长、并且不跑题，最好是在对地点进行简单的描写后，就以**个人游览顺序**来逐一描写这个地点的细节。也就是说，在粗略回答卡片上给的几个简单问题之后，就按个人“曾经”参观（未必要真去过）的顺序来描写。只要考官不叫停，考生就一直“走（说）”下去。这样，就能保证答案的长度和流畅度。

1．地点描写范文（An Historic Site）

I would like to describe a historic site in Beijing, which is often regarded as a fun place to go.

It is called The Grand Garden, which is famous for the *Dream of the Red Chamber*, one of the four ancient Chinese classic masterpieces. It was created between 1984 and 1989 in Beijing. Initially it was used as the film location for the TV series *Dream of Red Mansion*. It integrates artificial features and natural scenery into a harmonious whole. This garden has become an important tourist attraction in Beijing.

The first time that I went there is the first time that I came to Beijing fifteen years ago. I have seen many interesting sites in the garden, and it has been skillfully designed. It has various classical buildings, such as palaces, pavilions, courtyards, water features and rockeries as well as a nunnery. The first scene that I saw is a tall and huge gate with colorful delicately curved roof, which indicates that there are a lot to see in the garden, when I enter the gate, I can see a…

2．地点描写模板

开场白：

I would like to describe a place in ____________, which is often regarded as ____________.

简短介绍：

It is called ________________, which is famous for ______________________. It was built in ________________, 加简短描写。

所见所闻：

The ________ time that I want there is when _________. I have seen many ___________ sites there. For example, ___________, then ____________ 按个人游览顺序逐一描写，直到考官叫停为止。

二、练习

Describe a place near a lot of water that you enjoyed visiting.

You should say:

where this place was

what you did at this place

why you went there

and explain why you liked this place.

1．范文（Describe a place with a lot of water）

开场白：

I would like to describe a place near a lot of water, **which is often regarded as** one of the most attractive place for traveling in Beijing.

简短介绍：

It is called The Ming Tombs, **which is famous for** the tombs of 13 Ming Dynasty emperors, the tombs of seven concubines and the tomb of a eunuch there. **It was built** in the Ming Dynasty, beside which, there is a huge reservoir. According to UNESCO, the Ming Tombs' area was worthy of being listed as a World Heritage Site because it offers a number of unique attractions.

所见所闻：

The first time I went there is because I was asked to take a foreign professor to visit the place. Frankly speaking, when I knew that I was going to that place, I felt weird, because I preferred somewhere more relaxing. However, to my surprise, I had a good time there, because I have learnt much about Chinese culture. It is a good example of applying Fengshui, or geomancy. It showed the harmonious integration of remarkable architecture set in a natural environment.

For example, in front of the mausoleum of Emperor Yongle, there is a seven-kilometre-long colonnade, which is called the Sacred Way. This divine pathway is lined with willow trees, and as you make your way along the colonnade you stroll past life-size statues of camels, lions and elephants. You will also view statues of Chinese mythological beasts. And, as you reach the end of the Sacred Way you come across the statues of generals and other dignitaries.

2．举一反三

Describe a city that you have visited

You should say:

where the city was

when you went there

what you liked & disliked about the city

and explain what was special about this city.

Describe your favourite part of your hometown.

You should say:

where it is

how often you go there

what you do there

and explain why that is your favourite part of town.

Describe a place where you like to go shopping.

You should say:

what type of place it is

how often you go there

what kind of people work there

and explain why you like to shop at this place.

3. Related part 3 questions:

A Place with a Lot of Water

1. Why do people like places with a lot of water?
2. Do you think schools should teach children how to swim?
3. Do you think people use more water today than they did before ?
4. Do you think it's important to try to save water? (Why?)
5. Do you think it's necessary to control the amount of water that people use?
6. Do you think water is important?
7. Which location do you think uses more water, cities or rural areas?
8. Do you think water use will increase in the future or not?
9. How can people be made more aware of these problems?
10. Do you think increasing the cost of water will help conserve water?
11. Is there much clean water available in China?
12. Why do people in China like to go to places such as Hainan Island for a holiday?

A City You Have Visited or Lived in

1. What are the most important things that make a city worth living in?
2. What do you think are the advantages and disadvantages of living in a large city?
3. Do you think there are any possible health problems that could arise from living in a large city?
4. Do you think it's good for a child to live in a city?
5. Why do you think some cities are so crowded?
6. What do you suggest could be done to help alleviate this problem?
7. If you were planning a new city, what factors would you consider?
8. Compare the sounds that you hear in the city with what you can hear in the countryside.
9. Can you suggest any way that we could reduce the noise in the cities?

Your Favourite Part of Your Hometown

1. Which do you think is the better place to live, a city or the countryside? (Why?) Why do people today move from rural to urban areas?
2. Do you think this trend will continue in the future?
3. What would you say are the essential facilities and services that people need in their town or city?
4. What facilities are there for the welfare of old people in the community?
5. How do you think the facilities in your hometown could be improved?
6. Who should be responsible for providing these services and facilities?

A Place Where You Like to Go Shopping

1. Why do some people like shopping and others not like it?

2. What kinds of people dislike shopping? (Why?)
3. What kinds of places are there for shopping in your neighbourhood?
4. Compare big shops such as supermarkets & department stores with small shops.
5. Do you think the increase in the number of big supermarkets and department stores will cause the eventual disappearance of the small, family-owned shops?
6. Do you know any other way to do your shopping?
7. What are the advantages of internet shopping?
8. What are the different way that things are advertised?
9. What influence does advertising have on consumers?
10. Can you recall any examples of advertising aimed at children?

星期三

物体描写

物体描写常考话题如下：

1. An Important Letter
2. A Vehicle You Would Like To Own
3. A Work Of Art
4. A Family Photo
5. A Book You Enjoyed Reading
6. A Piece Of Furniture
7. A Book
8. A Book You Enjoyed as a Child
9. A Childhood Present
10. A Gift
11. A Piece Of Equipment
12. An Advertisement
13. A Car or Vehicle You Would Like to Have
14. Something that Helped You Learn a Language
15. Something You Made by Hand
16. A Photograph That You Like
17. Something You Would Like to Learn
18. Something You Want to Buy
19. A Childhood Song or Melody
20. A Childhood Toy
21. A Gift You Gave
22. A Good Law
23. A Magazine
24. A Newspaper You Like to Read
25. A Photograph
26. A Piece of Equipment
27. An Advertisement
28. An Old Thing in Your Family
29. Clothes

30. Something You Lost
31. Something You Saved For
32. Something You Made by Hand
33. A Work of Art
34. An Electrical/Electronic Product
35. An Email or Postcard
36. An Interesting Subject
37. Art or Music
38. Favourite Means Of Transportation
39. Clothing for Special Occasions
40. Your Favourite Subject at School

一、例题：A Childhood Toy

Describe a toy that was important to you in your childhood.

You should say:

when you got this toy

how you got this toy (or who gave you this toy)

how often you played with it

and explain why it was important to you.

儿童时期玩过的一个玩具，其实也就是一个物体描写题。根据前面的介绍，物体描写的思路应该是：

- 物体是什么（可以对外形稍加描写）
- 物体的功能或作用是什么
- 该物体和什么人相关（对物体描写结合人物或渗透情感，会让描写上一个台阶）
- 物体对所涉及人的影响

也就是说先简单介绍一下这个玩具，即什么时候、如何获得这个玩具的；然后介绍这个玩具的功能有哪些；接着用故事的形式把人物引进来，以便增加篇幅、引人入胜。最后，可以说说这个玩具对你个人产生了什么样的影响，这一点可多可少，可以灵活掌握。

1. 物体描写范文 1

I would like to describe an important toy that I played with in my childhood, which is an interesting doll that can speak English.

It is interesting, because in the doll, there is a computer chip, which enables the doll to "talk" like a baby. **For example**, if I press the button on her hand to wake her up, she would say, "Hi, mummy, I am hungry," and she would open and close her lips constantly, so that I can feed her some food. She swallowed the food, and after a while, she would excrete, and I have to clean it just like taking care of a baby. I don't know why, but it seems that I like it a lot, because I often kept doing it for hours.

Another reason that I like this doll is because it was sent to me as a birthday gift from my uncle, who loved me a lot and I did him much as well. Right now, we live far away, but the doll often reminds me of the good memories I have with him.

This doll played a very important role in my childhood, because it helped me to kill time and made me a responsible child. You know I am the only child at home, so I often felt lonely, but this doll enabled me to forget the dull time I had. And by taking good care of the doll, I have learnt to be considerate, and how important it is to care for others. So I would say, this is not only an interesting toy, but also a very important one.

2. 物体描写范文 2

When I was a child, I had numerous toys, but as for me, the most precious one is a tiny music box.

Modeled on a special train in San Francisco, this little music box is in the shape of a rectangle. The music box is brightly colored with a red car roof, dark green body and the words written in golden color. It's so delicate that I can even see the wooden chairs inside the special train. Up to now, I haven't found out the song the music box plays. However, the most exciting moment in my childhood was to see the metal keys up and down, performing the pure music from the paradise.

On the other hand, there's an interesting story behind that toy. On the day when I was leaving for America, my friend, Penny showed me an unclear picture of that special train, hoping me to take some real pictures of that strange vehicle. With her requests, not only did I take pictures, but bought a music box of that train for her, hoping to surprise her. However, when I took out the present, I was shocked to see Penny's music box which was exactly the same as mine. We were both happy, and our friendship had been strengthened since then.

Unfortunately, I lost contact with Penny as well as my music box because of moving to another place. But as the old saying "every music represents for a period of memory." Whenever I look at the place where my childhood toy used to be, the sweet melody and Penny's smile come back in my heart.

二、练习

Describe something you have made by hand

You should say:

what it was

where (and when) you made it

how you made it

and explain why you made it.

1. 范文

I would like to describe a kite I made when I was a kid. It is an eagle, which I learnt from my grandpa.

When I was a kid, flying kites was one of my favorite activities to do. My grandfather often made kites for me, but when I was about five years old, he taught me to make kites by myself. The first one, and the only one I have learnt to make is an eagle.

It needs delicate work, although the steps are easy. First of all, I draw a simple eagle on a piece of cloth, then I cut the edges, and make the cloth into the shape of an eagle, after which I make a framework by using very thin bamboo sticks. Then I tie the eagle on the bamboo framework. I mean to fasten the head, legs and wings of the eagle on the framework. Finally, I only need to tie it on a long string. The kite is done.

Since it was my first handicraft, and a corner stone of my growing up, so I did not fly the kite, instead I hung it on the wall of my room, and I had been praised for a long time.

I still keep that kite, because it is a memory of my childhood and my grandfather, since he passed away years ago. I miss him a lot.

2. 举一反三

Describe an antique or some other old thing that your family has kept for a long time.

You should say:

what it is

how (or when) your family first got this thing

how long your family has kept it

and explain why this thing is important to your family.

Describe a photograph that is important to you.

You should say:

Where you saw this photograph

what is in the photograph

when this photograph was taken

and explain why this photograph is important to you.

Describe an electrical (or electronic) machine or device you would like to buy.

You should say:

what special features you would like it to have

how you know about it

how you would use this thing

and explain why you would like to buy it.

3. Related part 3 questions

A Childhood Toy

1. What are the differences between the toys of boys and girls?
2. Why do some adults play toys?
3. What are the advantages of playing with toys?
4. Should all toys be educational?
5. What are the differences between handmade toys and electronic toys?

Something You Have Made by Hand

1. What are the reasons why people make handicrafts?
2. In general, how do people make handicrafts?
3. What are some differences between handmade things and things made by machine?
4. In what circumstances are handmade products more popular than factory-made products?

An Old Thing in Your Family

1. Which do you think is better, old things or new things?
2. As well as family photographs, what are some other things that people keep in their family for a long time?
3. Why do people pass these things onto the next generation?
4. Does the "old culture" (the traditions) of previous generations have much influence on your generation?
5. What do you think is better to display in a museum, old photographs or old things?

A photograph

1. Why do so many people like to take photographs?
2. What are the occasions when people take photographs?
3. Why do some people invade the privacy of celebrities by taking photographs of these celebrities?
4. Do you think news photographs are an important part of newspaper stories?
5. Do you think photographs are important in understanding (or representing or recording) history?
6. Compare old cameras with those in use today.
7. How can one distinguish between an old photograph and a recent one?
8. Compare the photos that professional photographers take and the photos that amateur photographers take.
9. Some people prefer to take still photographs while others prefer to take videos. Why?
10. Compare a typical family photograph and an artistic photograph.
11. Compare painting pictures and taking photographs (as art forms).
12. Which leaves a deeper impression on people, a picture or a written description of some event or scene?

星期四 事件描写

事件（event）描写是个考试难点，很多考生碰到这个话题都感到不知所措。有的是根本不知道该描写什么；有的是对相关事件了解太少，无从下手；也有考生有足够素材，但相关语言不会表达。其实，这个话题没有想象的那么难，但的确要做充足的准备。

目前最常考的事件题有：A Family Event；A Sports Event；A Public Event；A Recent Happy Event；A Happy Event；A Traditional Event in Your Country；A Local Event 等。下面就练习几个事件的描写。

一、例题：A Traditional Event

Describe an important traditional event in your country.

You should say:

what this event is

when it happens

who participates in this event and what they do

and explain why this is an important event in your country.

1. 审题、构思

事件的描写思路是：

- 什么事件
- 这个事件人们做什么
- 这个事件是怎么产生的
- 这个事件对人们（我）的影响是什么

2. 素材准备

春节之庙会	temple fair
元宵之灯笼展	lantern exhibition
端午之赛龙舟	dragon boat race
春节之放烟花	playing fire work
清明之扫墓	tomb sweeping
中秋之赏月	appreciate the moon

3. 事件描写范文

I would like to describe a traditional event in China. It is called the temple fair, which is a kind of social activity that is held on festive or specified days on the open ground in or near a temple.

It originated in ancient times when people offered sacrifices to the village god, which later gradually evolved into a marketplace for people to exchange products and a place for cultural performance. Farmers and merchants sell their farm produce, local specialties, and antiques, etc. craftsmen set up their stalls to show and sell their handicrafts and specialty snacks; folk artists establish a stage for singing, dancing, story-telling, etc. Ordinary people come to the temple fair to buy and sell goods, watch the performances, and sample snacks, giving the temple fair a bustling atmosphere.

Every Spring Festival, I would definitely go to a temple fair, because that is one of the rare places that I can feel the festival atmosphere, which reminds me of some of my childhood memories.

4. 事件描写模板

I would like to describe a traditional event in China. It is called（事件名称）..., which is a kind of social activity that is（简短介绍）....

It originated in（介绍起源） .., which later gradually evolved into.... 进一步解释这个事件人们干什么。这个事件的影响力。

二、练习

Describe an enjoyable family event that you attended.

You should say:

where and when this event took place

what happened at this event

who participated in this event

and explain why this event was enjoyable.

可以描写的素材：

wedding ceremony
birthday party
family trip
festival celebration
a baby was born
family reunion
funeral

1．范文

I would like to describe one of my family events, which took place about twenty years ago. It was a party celebrating my success of passing the college entrance exam.

You know, I was the first university student in my hometown, I mean a small village. Before me, no one had ever been to a university. So going to university was a dream for every villager, and I was the first to be successful. Therefore it was not only a big event for my family, it was a big event for the entire village.

Encouraged by the villagers, my parents decided to have a party. Everyone that we knew was invited, and all the villagers attended the party. It was really a big party. I was very moved, because I had never realized that my success of going into university was so important for the people in the village, they took me as a hero and an example for all young people there.

Every family gave me some money as a gift. I knew they had faith in me. I made my decision that I should study hard and try to make the village different.

With all the villagers' hope, I studied very hard, and graduated from university smoothly and got a decent job. I will always remember that family event.

2．举一反三

Describe a recent event that made you feel happy.

You should say:

what the event was

when and where it happened

who participated in this event

and explain why this event was so enjoyable.

Describe a public event that you attended.

You should say:

what the event was

when you went there

who you went there with

and explain why this event was so popular

Describe a sports event that you watched or took part in.

You should say:

when this event was held

where it was held

who participated in the event

and explain why you remember this event so well.

3. Part 3 questions related to events

1. What clothes do people traditionally wear in your country when celebrating traditional events and what food do they traditionally eat at these events?
2. Are young people as interested in traditional events as older people?
3. What traditions in China are disappearing or are in danger of disappearing?
4. How can old traditions be kept alive?
5. What traditions have already disappeared from Chinese culture and why did this happen?
6. Do you think that people tend to forget some (local) traditions when they move to a different place?
7. In general, how important are special family events, compared with public events?
8. Have there been any changes to typical family gatherings in China in the past few decades?
9. What would you say are the benefits to society of having sports events?
10. Why do you think some people who have a lot of money are still not happy?
11. Do you think there is any relationship between a person's happiness and their efficiency at work?

星期五 故事描写

讲故事应该是考生感觉最容易的，但讲好一个故事并不容易。最重要的是，很多考生不知道很多题其实就是一个故事。比如，一本书、一部电影、一个电视节目和一则新闻都是一个故事。只要考生恰当转换，就是一个简单的故事讲解。最常考的故事性话题有：

1. A Film
2. A Book You Would Like to Read Again
3. A Story from TV
4. An Interesting Film
5. The Latest Book You Have Read
6. A Newspaper or Magazine Article
7. Some Interesting News
8. A TV Program
9. Some Advice You Received

一、例题：The Latest Book You Have Read

> Describe a book you have read recently
>
> You should say:
>
> what book it was
>
> why you read it
>
> what you learned from this book
>
> and explain what you liked.

1. 审题、构思

描写一本书，其核心是一个故事。但是如果只描写书的故事情节，答案就会显得单一无趣，也不利于体现考生的口语水平。因此可以从以下几个方面去描写：

- 引出书名
- 介绍作者
- 描写情节
- 说明影响

2. 素材准备

（1）常见书名

The Call of the Wild	《野性的呼唤》
Wuthering Height	《呼啸山庄》
Pride and Prejudice	《傲慢与偏见》
Great Expectation	《远大前程》
Root	《根》
Out of Africa	《走出非洲》
Gone with the Wind	《飘》
A Farewell to Arms	《永别了，武器》
Jane Eyre	《简·爱》
Robinson Crusoe	《鲁滨逊漂流记》
The Paradise Lost	《失乐园》
Hamlet	《哈姆莱特》
Harry Potter	《哈利·波特》
Poor Dad and Rich Dad	《穷爸爸富爸爸》
《水浒传》	*Heroes of the Marshes; Outlaws of the Marsh*
《红楼梦》	*A Dream in Red Mansions*
《西游记》	*Journey to the West*
《三国演义》	*The Romance of the Three Kingdoms*
《史记》	*Records of the Grand Historian*
《西厢记》	*The Romance of West Chamber*
《聊斋志异》	*Strange Tales of a Lonely Studio*
《论语》	*Analects of Confucius*

（2）书的种类

cartoon, fairytales, fiction, nonfiction, science and fantasy, biography, love story, detective novel, romance

（3）名著简介

《水浒传》*Heroes of the Marshes; Outlaws of the Marsh*

China's great classic novel *Outlaws of the Marsh*, written in the fourteenth century, is a fictional account of twelfth-century events during the Song Dynasty. One by one, over a hundred men and women are forced by the harsh feudal officialdom to take to the hills. They band together and defeat every attempt of the government troops to crush them. Within this framework we find intrigue, adventure, murder, warfare, romance...in a connected series of fascinating individual tales, told in the suspenseful manner of the traditional storyteller.

《红楼梦》*A Dream in Red Mansions*

Also known as *The Story of the Stone*, this is arguably China's greatest literary masterpiece. It is mainly about the love story of two cousins and the history of a noble family from their prosperity to bankruptcy. The splendor of enchanting gardens, pleasure pavilions, and daily life of the most sophisticated refinements hides the realities of decay and self-destruction.

《三国演义》*The Romance of the Three Kingdoms*

The Romance of the Three Kingdoms is traditionally attributed to Luo Guanzhong, who lived sometime between 1315 and 1400 (late Yuan to early Ming period). Some scholars argue for an origin from around the second half of the fifteenth century (mid-Ming) based on characteristics of the text. It was written in partly vernacular and partly Classical Chinese and was considered the standard text for 300 years. The author made use of available historical records, including the *Records of the Three Kingdoms* compiled by Chen Shou, which covered events from the Yellow Turban Rebellion in 184 up to the unification of the three kingdoms under the Jin Dynasty in AD 280. The novel also includes material from Tang Dynasty poetic works, Yuan Dynasty operas and his own personal interpretation of elements such as virtue and legitimacy. The author combined this historical knowledge with a gift for storytelling to create a rich tapestry of personalities, and initially published it in 24 volumes.

This novel reflects the Confucian values that were prominent at the time it was written. According to Confucian moral standards, loyalty to one's family, friends, and superiors are important measures for distinguishing good and bad people.

《西游记》*Journey to the West*

Journey to the West is one of the Four Great Classical Novels of Chinese literature. Originally published anonymously in the 1590s during the Ming Dynasty, its authorship has been ascribed to the scholar Wu Cheng'en since the 20th century.

The novel is a fictionalised account of the mythologized legends around the Buddhist monk Xuanzang's pilgrimage to India (known as the Western Regions) during the Tang dynasty in order to obtain Buddhist religious texts called sūtras. The Bodhisattva Guan Yin, on instruction from the Buddha, the historical founder of Buddhism, gives this task to the monk and his three protectors in the form of disciples — namely Sun Wukong, Zhu Bajie and Sha Wujing — together with a dragon prince who acts as Xuanzang's steed, a white horse. These four characters have agreed to help Xuanzang as an atonement for past sins.

Journey to the West has a strong background in Chinese folk religion, Chinese mythology and value systems; the pantheon of Taoist immortals and Buddhist bodhisattvas is still reflective of some Chinese folk religious beliefs today.

Part of the novel's enduring popularity comes from the fact that it works on multiple levels: it is an adventure story, a dispenser of spiritual insight, and an extended allegory in which the group of pilgrims journeying toward India stands for the individual journeying toward enlightenment.

Gone with the Wind《飘》

Scarlett O'Hara is the daughter of an Irish immigrant who has risen from humble origins to become materially and socially successful in the deep south of 1861. He owns a plantation named Tara in Georgia. Scarlett is infatuated with Ashley Wilkes, who, although attracted to her (at least she thinks so), marries his cousin, Melanie Hamilton. Wilkes is genuinely ambiguous about his feelings toward Scarlett. He knows his feelings run deep, and are both emotional and sexual in nature; but he never resolves whether to act upon his feelings, or to renounce them and definitively reject Scarlett's flirtations, in favor of his wife and his social position. And though he never sins in the flesh, the novel clearly implies that he does so in his heart, leading Scarlett along; limited only by his weakness in making a decision as to what ultimately, he should do.

At the party announcing Ashley's engagement to Melanie, Scarlett meets Rhett Butler, who has a reputation as a rogue. As the Civil War begins, Scarlett accepts a proposal of marriage from Melanie's brother, Charles Hamilton, who soon dies of disease in training. Scarlett's main concern regarding his death is not grief but that she is required to wear black which she hates, and above all cannot attend parties. After the war, Scarlett inherits Tara and manages to keep the place going. When Scarlett cannot get money from Rhett to pay the taxes on Tara, she marries her sister's fiancé, Frank Kennedy, takes control of his business, and increases its profitability with business practices that make many Atlantians resent her. Frank is killed when he and other Ku Klux Klan members raid a shanty town where Scarlet was assaulted while driving alone. Remorseful after Frank's death, Scarlett marries Rhett, who is aware of her passion for Ashley(witnessed at Ashley and Melanie's engagement) but hopes that one day she will come to love him instead. Scarlett eventually comes to realize that she does love Rhett, but only once the couple has been through so much that Rhett has fallen out of love with her.

A Farewell to Arms《永别了，武器》

A Farewell to Arms is a semi-autobiographical novel written by Ernest Hemingway, first published in 1929. The novel is told through the point of view of Lieutenant Frederic Henry, an American serving as an ambulance driver in the Italian army during World War I.

The novel is about Hemingway's World War I experiences and his relationship with Agnes von Kurowsky in Milan. His wife Pauline underwent a caesarean section as Hemingway was writing about Catherine Barkley's childbirth.

On the surface, *A Farewell to Arms* is about the tragic romance between an American soldier Frederic Henry, and Catherine Barkley, a British nurse. Below the surface, the novel is about World War I and individual tragedy within the larger picture of greater tragedy. The novel portrays the cynicism of soldiers and the displacement of populations. Hemingway's stature as an American writer was secured with the publication of *A Farewell to Arms*.

Jane Eyre《简・爱》

Jane Eyre is a famous and influential novel by English writer Charlotte Brontë. It was published in London, England in 1847 by Smith, Elder & Co. with the title *Jane Eyre*. An

Autobiography under the pen name "Currer Bell".

Jane Eyre is a first-person narrative of the title character. The novel goes through five distinct stages: Jane's childhood at Gateshead, where she is emotionally and physically abused by her aunt and cousins; her education at Lowood School, where she acquires friends and role models but also suffers privations; her time as the governess of Thornfield Hall, where she falls in love with the Byronic employer, Edward Rochester; her time with the Rivers family at Marsh's End (or Moor House) and Morton, where her cold clergyman-cousin St. John Rivers proposes to her; and her reunion with and marriage to her beloved Rochester. Partly autobiographical, the novel abounds with social criticism. It is a novel considered ahead of its time. In spite of the dark, brooding elements, it has a strong sense of right and wrong, of morality at its core.

Robinson Crusoe《鲁滨逊漂流记》

Robinson Crusoe, is a novel by Daniel Defoe that was first published in 1719. The book is a fictional autobiography of the title character—a castaway who spends 28 years on a remote tropical island near Venezuela, encountering native Americans, captives, and mutineers before being rescued.

Crusoe joins an expedition to bring slaves from Africa, but he is shipwrecked in a storm about forty miles out to sea on an island (which he calls the Island of Despair) near the mouth of the Orinoco river on September 30, 1659. His companions all die. Having overcome his despair, he fetches arms, tools, and other supplies from the ship before it breaks apart and sinks. He proceeds to build a fenced-in habitation near a cave which he excavates himself. He keeps a calendar by making marks in a wooden cross built by himself, hunts, grows corn and rice, dries grapes to make raisins for the winter months, learns to make pottery, raises goats, etc., using tools created from stone and wood which he harvests on the island, and adopts a small parrot. He reads the Bible and suddenly becomes religious, thanking God for his fate in which nothing is missing but society.

Years later, he discovers native cannibals who occasionally visit the island to kill and eat prisoners. He helped a prisoner to escape, and name him "Friday". Crusoe then teaches him English and converts him to Christianity.

After another party of natives arrives to partake in a cannibal feast, Crusoe and Friday manage to kill most of the natives and save two of the prisoners. One is Friday's father and the other is a Spaniard, who informs Crusoe that there are other Spaniards shipwrecked on the mainland. A plan is devised wherein the Spaniard would return with Friday's father to the mainland and bring back the others, build a ship, and sail to a Spanish port. Before the Spaniards return, an English ship appears. Crusoe leaves the island.

3. 故事描写范文

I would like to describe a book I have read recently. It is called *A Dream in Red Mansions*,which is arguably China's greatest literary masterpiece. Actually, I should have read the book much earlier, but only till quite recently, have I got the time for it. And I love the book so much.

It was written by Cao Xueqin, who is the most famous novel writer in the Qing Dynasty.

The book is mainly about the love story of two cousins Jia Baoyu and Lin Daiyu, and the history of a noble family from their prosperous time to bankruptcy. By describing the splendor of enchanting gardens, pleasure pavilions, and daily life of the most sophisticated refinements, the writer is actually revealing the hidden realities of decay and self-destruction.

This book has great influence on me. For example, for the first time, I have enjoyed the beauty of Chinese language, I have never realized it can be so informative. Secondly, it helped to cultivate my interest in Chinese literature. Since then I have read many Chinese books. From each one I have benefited a lot.

4. 故事描写模板

I would like to describe a book I have read recently. It is called +书名，which is 简要介绍该书的地位。

It was written by 作者，who is one of the most …简要介绍作者。

The book is mainly about…描写情节。My favorite part is 细节描写一部分内容。

The book has great influence on me, for example 书对你的影响。

二、练习

Describe an interesting news you have heard.

You should say:

when it happened

where you got the news

what happened

and explain why you think it is interesting.

1. 范文

I would like to describe an interesting news I have heard the other day. I would like to entitle the news *the Ducks from the Ocean.*

I was told by one of my best friends, who is called a news hunter and spreader.

It was said that, one morning, in a bay of an American city, there were thousands of plastic ducks swimming to the coast, and many tourists were picking the ducks there. Many people questioned where these ducks come from. Latter, the same ocean experts told the public that the ducks were from a ship which wrecked a month ago, and the ship was carrying plastic toys to another country.

When I first heard the news, I felt interesting and fantastic, because nobody would anticipate the ducks coming to the coast. However, after a second thinking, I felt worried, because this news told us that we share the same ocean. If one part of the ocean is polluted, all the people around the ocean would be influenced sometime later, so if we want to protect the ocean, international cooperation is needed.

2. 举一反三

Describe a story you have seen from TV.

You should say:

When did you see it

What TV program it is from What it is about and explain how do you feel about the story.

Describe a well-known story from your country. You should say: who told you the story when you heard it what it was about and explain how you felt when you heard this story.

Describe a story happened on you or your friends. You should say: When it happened Who are involved What is the result and explain how it influenced you or your friends.

3. Related part 3 questions

The Latest Book You Have Read

1. Why do men and women choose to read different types of books?
2. Do you think it's a good idea for children to start learning how to read before they start school?
3. What is the role of the Internet in reading? Does it help to encourage people to read?
4. Do you think e-books will replace the way we read now?

Interesting News

1. What kind of news would be interesting?
2. Do you think the newspaper should attract readers by interesting news instead of more serious news?
3. Do you think newspapers will be replaced by the Internet?
4. Do you think it is important to keep one updated with the news?

星期六

活动描写

活动类题目的描写和故事相似，但更多是考生自己经历、参加或知道的一个活动。这些活动种类繁多。有课堂活动，也有业余活动等。常考的活动有：

1. A Class Or Course
2. A Walk
3. An English Class Activity
4. An Artistic Activity
5. A Party
6. A Leisure Activity
7. A Physical Activity
8. A Group Activity
9. A Childhood Activity
10. A New or Exciting Activity
11. A Childhood Game
12. A Performance
13. A Project or Homework Assignment
14. A Way to Relax
15. A Radio Program
16. An Exciting Sport
17. An Outdoor Activity

一、例题：Childhood Game

> Describe a game you enjoyed when you were a child.
> You should say:
> what the game was
> when, where and with whom you usually played it
> how you played it
> and explain why you enjoyed this game.

1. 审题、构思

活动（游戏）描写的思路：

- 活动（游戏）规则
- 活动（游戏）的影响力

2. 活动描写范文

开场白

I'd like to describe a game that I often played in my childhood, it's called "the Sand Bag", because the only tool of the game is a small sand bag.

活动（游戏）规则

It is easy to play, and generally it is played by many people. In the game, all the players will be divided into two groups, one group would stand in the middle of a square, while the other would stand on both sides of the first group, and throw a small sand bag to the people in the middle trying to hit the people. So for the people in the middle, they will have to be swift, and try not to be hit or even touched by the sand bag, if they were, they were "killed" and would have to get out of the game, the game would not be over until the last one in the group was killed. However, if they can catch the sand bag, they saved one member of their group.

活动（游戏）的影响力

I often played that game when I was a child, because it can be played anywhere and everybody can play it. More importantly, it is a good way to help the children to build up their body, because they would have to run a lot, and it is also a good team building game. I have made many good friends by this game at that time. I loved the game, and I still keep some sand bags that I have made by myself, it often reminds me of my childhood.

3. 活动描写模版

开场白

I would like to describe a game that I often played in my childhood, it is called ______________. It is called so because _____________

活动（游戏）规则

It is easy to play, and generally it is played by many people. In the game+简单描写活动（游戏）规则。

活动（游戏）的影响力

I often played that game when I was a child, because+活动（游戏）影响力，可以谈这个游戏从整体上对孩子们的影响，并具体谈对你自己的影响。可以说对身心健康的正面影响，还可以从团队精神，童年回忆等方面来谈。

二、练习

Describe a leisure activity you often do.

You should say:

what activity it is

what equipment you need to use

who you do it with

and explain why you like this activity.

1. 范文

开场白

I would like to describe an activity that I often do, it is called ‘Idiom Dragon’ or ‘Idiom Chain’. It is called so because many idioms will be named out and make a long long chain.

活动（游戏）规则

It is interesting to play, and generally it can be played by many people, the more the better, although there is no limit on the number of players. In the game, all the players will have to think and tell many idioms. The first speaker starts the game by naming out an idiom which is a four-character fixed expression. Then the second speaker has to name out another idiom starting with the last character of the idiom the previous player give. And now it moves on and stops when someone can not move , and he or she would have to sing a song, tell a joke, or do something he or she is good at.

活动（游戏）的影响力

We often played that game when we were having a party or something. This game often brings us much fun, because there are always good idioms given out and we can enjoy the songs and jokes if somebody failed. More importantly, this help us to get to know the people around better, and it helps to develop the friendship among us. It left us many good memories.

2. 举一反三

Describe a picnic or meal that you ate outdoors.
You should say:
  where you had this meal
  who was with you
  what you ate and drank
and explain why you ate outdoors.

Describe a show or performance that you enjoyed watching.
You should say:
  what kind of performance it was
  when and where you saw it
  who you saw it with
and explain why you attended this performance.

Describe a party you would like to arrange for your friends.
You should say:
  who you would invite to the party
  when and where you would hold the party
  what you would do at the party
and explain why you would hold this party.

3. Related part 3 questions

Leisure Time Activities

1. Do you think it's important for students and working people to have some leisure time?
2. Why do you think some people are interested in a certain leisure activity or hobby while other people are interested in different leisure time activities?
3. How important do you think it is to preserve the traditional leisure time activities in your culture?
4. Some parents think that their children should spend all of their time on study and no time on leisure activities. Do you agree?

Parties

1. On what occasions do people in China come together for family gatherings?
2. Do you personally feel that traditional celebrations/festivals are important?
3. Has the way that people celebrate traditional festivals changed at all in the past few decades?
4. From your knowledge of traditional celebrations in other countries, what differences do you see between these foreign festivals and those in your culture?

Eating Out

1. In what ways is eating at home different to eating in a restaurant?
2. Have there been any changes over the past 30 years in what Chinese people eat?
3. In your opinion, what is a "healthy diet" and what is an "unhealthy diet"?
4. Do you think the government has a responsibility to inform people about what is and what isn't a healthy diet?
5. Can you suggest any way to make traditional food more attractive?

星期日

经历描写

经历类的描写，就是讲述考生自己经历过的故事。只是，自己是主人翁，相对而言更接近考生的日常生活。但很多考生在碰到这些题目的时候，发现自己素材不够，或者说没有这样类似的经历，因此感觉无从下手。考生需要在进考场前，准备好相关素材，以防考试冷场。常考的经历类话题有：

1. An Important Decision
2. A Busy Time
3. Receiving A Large Sum Of Money
4. An Unhappy Shopping Experience
5. A Meal For Your Friends
6. An Interesting Or Unusual Thing You Did Recently
7. A Happy Childhood Memory
8. A Lesson, Class or Training Session
9. A Positive Change
10. A Recent Change
11. A Stage of Your Life
12. A Trip You Made
13. A Long Journey you had
14. A Special Meal you had
15. An Occasion When You Were Late
16. Leisure Time
17. Last Weekend
18. A Conversation You Had
19. A Journey with Your Friends
20. A Recent Change
21. A Stage in Your Life you Enjoyed
22. A Time When You Helped Someone
23. A Success You Have Had
24. A Time When You Helped Someone
25. A Picnic or Outdoor Meal you had
26. A Future Change
27. A Healthy Habit you had

28. A Job you did
29. A Letter or Card You Received
30. A Job You Did Quickly
31. A Piece of Good News you received by Phone
32. A Skill You Recently Learned
33. A Science Lesson
34. An Educational Trip
35. Living in a Place in Another Country
36. School Holidays you had
37. Studying IELTS
38. Your Favourite Season
39. Some Recent News
40. An Important Letter You Wrote
41. A Traffic Jam you experienced
42. A Sport You Played in Childhood
43. The Perfect Climate you have experienced
44. Future Work Plans you have made
45. An Interesting Talk you have heard
46. A Practical Skill you have learnt
47. A Foreign Culture you have learnt

一、例题：An Occasion When You Were Late

> Describe an occasion when you were late.
> You should say:
> when this happened
> what occasion you were late for
> why you were late
> and explain what happened as a result of your lateness.

1. 审题、构思

迟到的场合有：面试；约会；赶车；参加聚会；参加婚礼；上班迟到；上学迟到等。
迟到的理由有：睡过了；记错时间了；堵车了；路上碰到人或事了；被其他事情耽误了等。

2. 答题思路

- 背景介绍
- 迟到原因
- 处理办法
- 后果影响

3. 经历描写范文

开场白

I'd like to describe one of my experiences of being late. I was late for a train.

背景介绍

You know, I am always busy, and I seldom have time to relax. Last summer, I finally made a decision to go to Shanghai for a trip, because I wanted to reward myself for five continuous hard-working days. I bought a train ticket, and it was about 9 o'clock in the morning.

迟到原因

I packed in the evening, got washed and went to bed much earlier than usual, because I wanted to have a good sleep and be more energetic for travelling. However, things did not go as planned. I could not sleep at all, I tried my best to fall asleep, but I couldn't help thinking about what to do on the trip. At one o'clock in the morning, I was still awake, so I gave up, and decided to get up and watch a movie, because I was very frustrated at that moment. I watched a movie, but did not remember the time when I fell asleep on the couch. When I wake up, it was in the morning. I was almost mad when I saw my clock on the wall, it was eight thirty.

处理办法

It was impossible for me to catch the train in thirty minutes but I did not give up, I carried my bags and rushed out. I took a taxi, although I planned to take a bus. When I arrived at the railway station, it was nine thirty, I was very upset, I went to the ticket window, attempting to get refund for my ticket and buy a ticket for the next train.

后果影响

When I explained what had happened, the kind ticket seller told me that I did not need to buy a new ticket, because my train was delayed, and I was just in time. I was very surprised and extremely excited. I got on the train, and had a nice journey and a memory.

4. 经历描写模板

开场白

I'd like to describe one of my experiences of being late. It was late for ____________________.

背景介绍

You know, I +迟到前的情况。

迟到原因

将迟到的原因用故事的形式叙述出来。

处理办法

I did many things to make up, you know, I ….

后果影响

在介绍结果的时候，最好能出人意料，不要落于俗套，给自己的故事增加一点趣味性。

二、练习

Describe an interesting trip that you made.

You should say:

when and where you went

why you went there

how you traveled

and explain why this trip was interesting.

1. 范文

开场白

I'd like to describe one of my traveling experiences. It was last summer when I went to Hainan to meet my online girlfriend.

背景介绍

You know, I quite like surfing the Internet. I often make friends online. I have been chatting with a girl on Skype for a long time, and we found much in common and gradually I felt in love with her, and we decided to meet and I went to Hainan to visit her.

所见所闻

I have never seen her. I was very anxious and even nervous, because I was not sure what would happen. When I arrived there, I called her and asked her out. She said yes immediately and asked me to wait for her at a landmark. However, I was very surprised and embarrassed when she came. Because she was not alone, her whole family came out, later she had told me that she had told her family that I was going to visit her, and all her family members were curious and would like to see me so that they can help to decide if I was the right man for her. Insisted by her family, I went to her family, and I met everyone in her family, they were all very nice, but I was scared.

解释理由

I quite liked her; actually I liked her more when I saw her. She is beautiful and elegant, but I was not ready at that moment to see her family, however, her family thought she should take it seriously when meeting a guy.

后果影响

I had a nice day there and said goodbye to everyone the next day, I came back and told this to my family and friends. Everyone was amazed; they said that I was lucky, because my experience is quite like a movie. I have to admit that I did have a nice time and a nice journey, because it made my life different.

2. 举一反三

Describe a science lesson that you had in school.

You should say:

when you attended this lesson

where you attended this lesson

what you learned

and explain how you learned it.

Describe a happy memory from your childhood. You should say: what the memory is when it happened who was with you and explain why it is a happy memory.

Describe a success you have had. You should say: what it was when it happened how easy or difficult it was to achieve and explain how important this success was.

3. Related part 3 questions

Punctuality

1. What are some of the common excuses that people give when they are late?
2. Are people in China usually punctual when they have to be somewhere at a certain time?
3. For what situations is being on time very important?
4. Do you think modern technology gives us more time, or less?
5. Do you think the current working hours of most people are reasonable?

Science and Technology in Society

1. What do you think is the greatest scientific discovery of the 21st century?
2. What effects does rapid technological change have on people in society?
3. Can you think of any example of technology that are not good for society?
4. Do you think it's good for schools to have science classes?
5. Do you think it's suitable to start teaching science to very young children?
6. Can you think of any example of learning about science outside of the classroom?
7. Why do you think more males than females study science?
8. Who do you think should finance scientific research, government or private companies?
9. Do you think new scientific knowledge should be freely shared by different countries?

Childhood

1. What can adults learn from looking back at their own childhood?
2. Some adults think that childhood was the best part of their lives. Why do they think that way?
3. What are some things that people keep from their childhood?
4. Can you think of any way to enhance one's memory in order to increase one's learning capacity?
5. What do you think is the value of teaching history in school?

6. Do you think it is a good idea to use audio-visual materials such as video or films to make the subject of history seem more interesting?

Success

1. How would you define the word "success"?
2. In your society, how is a person's social status evaluated?
3. Do you think "success" is the same as making a lot of money?
4. In recent years, have people's ideas about success changed in China?
5. How do you think a person can become "successful" in life?
6. There are some people who do not achieve success despite having the qualities or doing what you've just said. Why do you think that is?
7. How can a person become successful at his or her job?
8. How can a boss make his or her employees feel successful?
9. Do you think someone who doesn't really like his or her job is still able to become successful in that job?

4周攻克

雅思口语周计划

第四周　7天冲刺：掌握7大考试难点

本周学习目标：

本周为周计划最后一周，也就是冲刺周。本周主要突破雅思口语考试的7个难点，也就是常考的7个有难度的话题和口语考试第三部分的7大考点。这7个话题分别是：animal，restaurant，law，building，course，change，job这7个话题在口语一、二、三部分都经常考到，因此它们都是重点，但是，关于这些话题的问题，往往刁钻古怪，让考生不知如何作答，从而影响考试的整体得分。为了解决这个问题，本周每天都详细解决一个话题，在深入学习这些话题的同时，也希望考生能同时掌握回答关于：动物、场所、法律、建筑物、课程、人生变化和工作的所有问题，做到举一反三。

星期一

IT'S ALL ABOUT ANIMALS

今天首先要深入学习关于动物的第 1、2、3 部分的常考问题。其中第 1 部分的话题包括：animals，birds，pets；第 2 部分学习描写 an interesting animal；第 3 部分讨论与动物相关的抽象问题。通过学习这些问题的范文和讲解，希望考生能沉着应对雅思口语考试关于动物的所有问题。

一、首先请根据下面的题目自测

Part 1	**Topic 1 Animals** 1. What's your favourite animal? 2. Are you afraid of any animals? 3. What wild animals can you see in your hometown? 4. Do you eat animals? **Topic 2 Birds** 1. Do you like birds? 2. What are the birds that you can see in your hometown? 3. Do any birds have any particular significance in China? 4. Do you think birds should be protected? **Topic 3 Pets** 1. Do you keep pets at home? 2. What are the common pets in China? 3. Why do you think people like keeping dogs? 4. What do you think is the biggest problem when taking care of a pet?
Part 2	Describe an interesting animal you have seen. You should say: what animal it was where you saw it what happened when you saw it and explain why you thought it was interesting. **wrap-up questions:** ● Have you seen it later?
Part 3	**Questions related to animals** 1. How can animals help people? 2. Do you think it is necessary to have pet hospitals? 3. Do you think it's a good idea to use a leash when taking your dog outside for a walk? 4. What do you think is the value of pets?

（续）

Part 3	5. Some people say that people are more important than animals. What do you think? 6. What's your opinion of people who put birds in cages? 7. What do you think are the benefits of having zoos? 8. Is the government doing anything to protect wild animals in China? 9. What do you think is the value of protecting endangered animals? 10. Do you agree that animals should be used for scientific testing of chemical products such as new medicines?

二、模板答案

Part 1

Topic 1 Animals

1. What's your favourite animal?

— Well, actually I am a typical animal lover. I like many animals, but my favorite is still dogs. Because I have kept many dogs at home, they are my best friends.

2. Are you afraid of any animals?

— Frankly speaking, yes. I am allergic to spiders, and I am also sick of seeing huge snakes. I think they look evil, and I have heard many stories about how they attack and kill humans.

3. What wild animals can you see in your hometown?

— I am from a mountain area in Hubei Province, so I can see many animals there, such as hares, boars.

4. Do you eat animals?

— Well, I do not eat wild animals, but I am not a vegetarian, so I eat pork, beef and mutton, although I do not kill them myself.

Topic 2 Birds

1. Do you like birds?

— Yes, I do, I love them. I think they are the most beautiful creatures in the world.

2. What are the birds that you can see in your hometown?

— Well, there are many kinds of birds in my hometown. For example, there are many black birds, sparrows and swallows. Oh, magpie is everywhere.

3. Do any birds have any particular significance in China?

— Yes, there are many birds get special meaning. For example, in the early morning, if you see a magpie singing around, it means you will have good luck that day, but if you come across a crow, you'd better stay at home, because it is generally believed that bad luck is waiting for you.

4. **Do you think birds should be protected?**

— Yes, definitely, because the number of birds has decreased greatly in the last several years, and human activities are threatening more birds, if actions not taken, many birds would be extinct soon, and that would be great loss for the world.

Topic 3 Pets

1. **Do you keep pets at home?**

— Yes, I have many dogs at home. I was the only child at home, so I grew up with dogs actually.

2. **What are the common pets in China?**

— Well, different people may keep different pets, but generally speaking, dogs, cats, and birds are still the most common ones, because they are generally easy to keep.

3. **Why do you think people like keeping dogs?**

— Well, it is hard to say, but for me, dogs are easy to keep, and they are very faithful, so they can bring me a lot of happiness, sometimes, dogs can even help to do some simple things, and some can even be the guard.

4. **What do you think is the biggest problem when taking care of a pet?**

— The biggest problem is time. It is very time consuming to keep a pet. Take dogs for example, you have to feed them, wash them and take them out for walks, and you also need to talk to them so that they would not feel lonely. Very often, you have to take them to the hospital. It needs a lot of time.

Part 2

Describe an interesting animal you have seen. You should say: what animal it was where you saw it what happened when you saw it and explain why you thought it was interesting.

Warp-up questions:

- Have you seen it later?

描写动物的思路和人物描写大同小异，也就是从外貌特征、性格特点、故事、影响等方面来进行描写。

I would like to describe a very interesting dog I have seen in a park last winter. I was sitting on a bench to wait for my friends, and there were many dogs playing around. There is one dog that was very eye catching.（开场白）

It was pure bright, by looking at its face, it looks like a fox, but I did not know its feed. The owner called it “snow Ball”, I think it deserves the name. It is rather small, and it looks very interesting. You know, it was wearing a red waist coat, and four leather shoes, more interestingly, on its head, there was a red head dress, which made her looked like an elegant lady. Because of that, it was very popular among the dogs, and all the people there liked her a lot.（外貌描写）

It seems that the dog knows her popularity, because she showed a lot of her talents. It stood up and danced with her owner, and barked rhythmically as if she knew music. She also rolled on the grassland and caused a lot of laughter around.（故事支持）

I loved that dog, and I recorded a short video for her play and showed that to my dogs latter, and my dogs barked at my camera, seems want to play with her.（后续，也可以谈它对我的影响）

Part 3 Questions related to animals

1. How can animals help people?

—In my opinion, animals help people a lot. It is not exaggerating to say that humans rely on animals. Because first of all, animals provide food to humans; and they, if well trained, help people to do much work; some animals even save people's lives, and make people spiritually good.

2. Do you think it is necessary to have pet hospitals?

— Pet hospitals are extremely necessary, because pets may get sick, and only professional doctors can save them. If the sick pets are not treated in time, they may spread disease to other animals and even humans, so pet hospitals are equally important with human hospitals.

3. Do you think it's a good idea to use a leash when taking your dog outside for a walk?

— Well, I think it is rather cruel to do that, because we limit the freedom of animals, but we have no choice, because some animals may attack passersby.

4. What do you think is the value of pets?

— There are numerous values of pets, but here I can only name out several of them. Firstly, pets accompany those lonely elder people and bring them happiness. Secondly, pets can be educational, because they can help to make the children responsible; what's more, some pets can help the disabled people.

5. Some people say that people are more important than animals. What do you think?

— I am afraid I cannot agree with that statement, because animals are just like humans, they are one part of the world. It is totally wrong and selfish to take human as the center of the world, and it is even more unreasonable to sacrifice animals for humans.

6. What's your opinion of people who put birds in cages?

— I think they are fake "bird lovers". They keep birds not because they like them, but because birds can help them to kill time. This is unfair, the birds need freedom. I would say, if people really love birds, they should give them that freedom.

7. What do you think are the benefits of having zoos?

— Frankly speaking, I hate going to the zoo. It makes me feel bad to see the encaged animals, they are so pitiful, they are supposed to be in the wild where they can enjoy their life. However, at the same time, I have to say, zoo is a good place to teach people to love animals and protect them.

8. Is the government doing anything to protect wild animals in China?

— Yes, the Chinese government has done a lot to protect wild animals. First of all, many animal laws are issued, so the people who kill or abuse animals would get punished. Secondly, animal protection skills are seen in the textbooks, so all the students' awareness of animal protection would be raised. Also, we can see many non-profit advertisements about animal protection.

9. What do you think is the value of protecting endangered animals?

— Any species in the world have a role to play, so it is very important to guarantee their existence, if some animals are extinct, the food chain will be broken, then humans would be in great trouble. Also, the endangered animals are important resources for researches, they can tell us more about the history of the world. So it is rather important to make sure that they would not die out.

10. Do you agree that animals should be used for scientific testing of chemical products such as new medicines?

— It is very hard to say, because it is unfair to sacrifice the animals for human benefits. But, scientific testing is necessary, and it is unfair to do experiments on humans, so testing on some animals is a compromise. And for some tests, they are not only for humans, but also for animal protection. So animal testing, if it is used in the right way, is acceptable.

星期二

IT'S ALL ABOUT PLACES

今天首先要深入学习关于地方的第 1、2、3 部分的常考问题。其中第 1 部分的话题包括：restaurant，parks，gardens；第 2 部分学习描写 a cafe or restaurant；第 3 部分讨论与 restaurant 相关的抽象问题。通过学习这些问题的范文和讲解，帮助考生回答关于地方话题的所有问题。

一、首先请根据下面的题目自测

Part 1	**Topic 1 Restaurants** 1. Do you usually go out to eat or do you usually eat at home? 2. What skills do people need to work in a restaurant? 3. What are the qualities of a good restaurant? **Topic 2 Parks and public gardens** 1. Are there many parks or public gardens where you live? 2. Do you think parks and public gardens are important to a city? (Why?/Why not?) 3. What do you like to do when you go to a park or public garden? 4. What do other people do in these places? **Topic 3 Garden** 1. Does your family have a garden? 2. Do many people in China have their own garden? 3. If someone has a private garden in China, do they usually prefer to grow flowers or vegetables?
Part 2	Describe a cafe or restaurant that you know. You should say: where it is how often you go there what kind of food they serve there and explain why you like to eat at this place. **wrap-up questions:** ● Do you think other people would like to go to this restaurant?
Part 3	**Questions related to restaurant** 1. What are some of the factors that make a restaurant a good one? 2. What are the most popular kinds of restaurant in China today? 3. How have restaurants in China changed in the last few years? 4. How is restaurant food different to home cooking? 5. Do you think multi-national restaurant companies such as KFC are changing the food culture of China?

二、模板答案

Part 1

Topic 1 Restaurants

1. **Do you usually go out to eat or do you usually eat at home?**

— Well, I do not eat out a lot, because my parents cook me very tasty food, and I often found the food in the restaurant unclean.

2. **What skills do people need to work in a restaurant?**

— I think, to be a qualified waiter or waitress, one need to be patient, because she or he may come across all kinds of people, some may not be very nice. Also, a waiter or waitress needs to be smart, I mean, when busy, he or she still needs to handle things well.

3. **What are the qualities of a good restaurant?**

— As I see it, a good restaurant means they can provide good service. So first of all, it needs to be clean and safe, that's the top priority. In addition, a good restaurant needs to provide customers with good environment, so that they can enjoy the food there. The most important quality is to provide good food and service so that people can come back again.

Topic 2 Parks and public gardens

1. **Are there many parks or public gardens where you live?**

— Yes, there are several small parks and green areas around, so I often go there for a walk after dinner. I also read there sometimes.

2. **Do you think parks and public gardens are important to a city? (Why?/Why not?)**

— Sure, I would compare them as the lung of the city, because they give out the fresh air we need and also they provide a public place for everybody to go, where people can make friends.

3. **What do you like to do when you go to a park or public garden?**

— Generally I go there for walks, so that I can get some fresh air, sometimes, in the weekend, I would like to go there to chat with friends or do some reading.

4. **What do other people do in these places?**

— There are many people, like me, who go for a walk, and in the early morning and evening, there would be many people dancing there. There are also many people just sitting around to relax.

Topic 3 Garden

1. **Does your family have a garden?**

— No, not now, years ago, I lived in the country side, we had a big garden, but now I live in an apartment with my family, so it is impossible to have a garden, but I do keep some plants at home.

2. **Do many people in China have their own garden?**

— Well, it depends on where people live, people in big cities like Beijing cannot afford a garden, but people in the rural area or outskirts of the cities may have gardens.

3. **If someone has a private garden in China, do they usually prefer to grow flowers or vegetables?**

— In China, we can see food in almost every corner, so we can see vegetables in many gardens, but there are still some flowers in the garden.

Part 2

Describe a cafe or restaurant that you know. You should say: where it is how often you go there what kind of food they serve there and explain why you like to eat at this place.

wrap-up questions:

● Do you think other people would like to go to this restaurant?

描述一个餐馆或咖啡厅，无非就是从其外部装修，内部设计，饮食，服务，环境，价格等方面来说。

I'd like to describe a very good restaurant that I often go to, it's a Sichuan(spicy food) style restaurant, which is located very close to the North Third Ring Road in Beijing.

I went there for the first time three years ago, I went there with a friend. I was attracted by it from the first sight. It was in an old building with lanterns. It looked very cozy. When I first approached it, there were two good looking ushers greeting us in the traditional way.

Soon, we were led to a table close to the window, from where we could see the night view of the street. The decoration in the restaurant is very special, the ceiling of the room was curved with flying dragons and phoenix, and poles were all red. On the wall, there are some old pictures and some Chinese paintings, which are of my style.

More importantly, I love the food there, and all the waitress there are very professional, so I had a very nice dinner there. So I always go there whenever I invite friends for a dinner. I think you should go and have a try. You will love it.

周计划提示

可用素材：

dim light, candle night	昏暗的灯光或者烛光，营造浪漫氛围
light music	轻音乐，让人感觉温馨
variety show during the dining time	一边吃饭，一边欣赏表演

discount	折扣，价格合理
free drinks for ladies	为女生提供免费软饮
free parking	免费停车
umbrella available in rainy days	雨天免费提供雨具

以上这些都是让一个餐馆变得有吸引力的素材，随便挑选几个，就能成功描述一个餐馆。

Part 3 Questions related to restaurants

1. **What are some of the factors that make a restaurant a good one?**

— Well, I think there are many factors that may contribute to a good restaurant, first of all, the food needs to be good, and the price reasonable. Also the environment needs to be cozy, so that people may feel like coming back again. What's more, the service should be considerable. （参考以上信息，随意挑取几个来回答即可）

2. **What are the most popular kinds of restaurant in China today?**

— Well, that is hard to say, because China is a big place, and each place may have its own situation, but in Beijing, I have found that the restaurants which provide spicy food, hot pot and western food are popular, because they provide the food of good taste and specialty.

3. **How have restaurants in China changed in the last few years?**

— Like anything else, restaurants in China have gone through great changes. First of all, the management is more formal and professional, there are many university graduates who have taken part in restaurant management, but traditionally, restaurants are family based. Also, there is more diversity and chefs are more creative than usual, so that the needs of the customers are better met.

4. **How is restaurant food different to home cooking?**

— Restaurant food and homemade food are different in many aspects. Firstly, there is more variety in restaurant, but the food at home is cleaner. The food in restaurants is cooked by using more ingredients, and homemade food is more economical.

5. **Do you think multi-national restaurant companies such as KFC are changing the food culture of China?**

— Well, yes, but I would like to take it this way, Chinese food culture and international restaurants are having amutual influence. The management concept of western restaurants is influencing Chinese restaurants a lot, but restaurants from other countries are borrowing the tastes of Chinese restaurants, for example, KFC made its Chicken burger rather spicy.

星期三

IT'S ALL ABOUT LAW

今天主要学习关于法律的常考问题。其中第1部分的话题包括：age，crime，police；第2部分学习描写a good law；第3部分讨论与法律相关的抽象问题。通过学习这些问题的范文和讲解，帮助考生回答关于法律话题的所有问题。

一、首先请根据下面的题目自测

Part 1	**Topic 1 Age** 1. At what age, can people get married in China? 2. Is there any limit on age for people to drink? **Topic 2 Crime** 1. What is the most common crime in your area? 2. What crime is the most serious one for China? 3. Do you think criminals should be sent to prison? 4. Do you think the criminals who killed others should be killed? **Topic 3 Police** 1. Do people in China like the police? 2. What kinds of people are interested in working as police officers? 3. What are the working conditions of the police like? 4. Why do you think there are more policemen than there are policewomen?
Part 2	Describe a good law in your country. You should say: what the law is how you first learned about this law who benefits from this law and explain why you think this is a good law. **wrap-up questions:** 1. Would you say this law is suitable for other countries? 2. Do other people also think this is a good law?
Part 3	**Questions related to law** 1. What role does law play in society? 2. If there were no laws, what do you think society would be like? 3. What do you think of China's "One Child Policy"? Is it a good law in your opinion? 4. What is the difference between a policy and a law? 5. Do you think all laws are fair? 6. In many cultures there are stories about people who "rob from the rich to give to the poor". Do you think it's suitable to tell this kind of story to children?

（续）

Part 3	7. Do you think it's morally right to have a death penalty? 8. Do you think most people in China abide by the law? 9. Can you suggest any way to solve the problem of people breaking the law? 10. What benefits are there for society when people obey the law? 11. Why do you think some people break the law? 12. How do you think the police and lawyers play different roles in connection to law? 13. What are the benefits of having international laws? 14. If there were no international laws, what do you think the world would be like? 15. Do you think it is suitable to have the same laws for every country?

二、模板答案

Part 1

Topic 1 Age

1. **At what age, can people get married in China?**

— According to the marriage law, men can get married at 22, and women can get married at 20.

2. **Is there any limit on age for people to drink?**

— Frankly speaking, I am not sure if there is a law to control alcohol in youth, but there are many young people who drink. And generally, parents and teachers would not allow the young people to drink.

Topic 2 Crime

1. **What is the most common crime in your area?**

— Generally speaking, the area I live in is very safe, but I was told that some people have been accused of stealing. I guess that is the most common one.

2. **What crime is the most serious one for China?**

— Well, to be frank, I am not sure about that, because I get no access to that kind of information, but I think cheating and robbery can be often seen in the media, so I think that may be they are the most serious ones.

3. **Do you think criminals should be sent to prison?**

—Well, that is hard to say. But I personally prefer to make the criminals work, because putting them into prison means people have to feed them, which is not punishment at all, they should make some contribution to society.

4. **Do you think the criminals who killed others should be killed?**

— I would say yes, killing the death criminals is not only to punish those who kill others, but also take it as a warning, so that people would not kill others easily.

Topic 3 Police

1. **Do people in China like the police?**

— Generally speaking, the police are very much respected, because the education system has beautified their image. However, in reality, there are many police who are very bad. I do not like them much.

2. **What kinds of people are interested in working as police officers?**

— I don't know, but I guess those who like challenges and enjoy adventures.

3. **What are the working conditions of the police like?**

— The police work in very tough conditions, because most of them work outside. In order to finish their tasks, they will have to stand the very difficult physical conditions.

4. **Why do you think there are more policemen than there are policewomen?**

— I think because of the nature of their work. Generally, there are more male criminals than female ones, so there is more need for policeman. And as I said before that police work in very hard conditions, so not many women would like to choose that career.

Part 2

Describe a good law in your country.
You should say:
what the law is
how you first learned about this law
who benefits from this law
and explain why you think this is a good law.

wrap-up questions:

1. Would you say that this law is suitable for other countries?
2. Do other people also think this is a good law?

The law I am going to introduce is, I am not sure what it is called, but it is about compulsory education. According to this law, every child in China has the right to get education for at least nine years, because all the children can get free education for nine years, so all the parents are obliged to send their children to school, if not, the parents will be fined.

I got to know about this during my traveling in a remote area. There was a family that was very poor, and the parents wanted their children to stay at home to help to do some housework, but they could not do that. I was very glad to know that we have such a law.

Because I think education is very important for every child. Without a certain amount of education, children will not be able to make a living, and more importantly, only if every child gets education, can the quality of the people be improved, and only in that way, the economy of the country can be developed.

So I would say, this law is very good, not only for those children who get education, but also for the whole nation.

Part 3 Questions related to law

1. **What role does law play in society?**

   — I think law plays a very important role in society. It is the law that makes the society safe and stable, because the law requires people to behave under the law system, so the people have to behave themselves.

2. **If there were no laws, what do you think society would be like?**

   — Well, I can never imagine what would happen if there was no law. Maybe the world will be in a mess, because that would mean people can just do whatever they want, and the physically strong ones would always have an advantage. The weak ones would have to suffer, so there would be no good or bad, only the strong would live and the weak would die.

3. **What do you think of China's "One Child Policy"? Is it a good law in your opinion?**

   — Well, since China is overpopulated, which has brought the country and the world a lot of troubles, especially in terms of natural resources and living spaces. It is vitally important for the Chinese government to do something to control the population. But, as any other policy, it has both advantages and disadvantages, the one child policy has caused many problems, such as spoiled children ect.

4. **What is the difference between a policy and a law?**

   — Frankly speaking, I am not sure about that, but I guess a policy tells people the direction (where and how people should do), while the law punishes those who violated it. Hence it warns the people not to break the law.

5. **Do you think all laws are fair?**

   — That's impossible, as the old saying goes, there is no fairness in laws, because in real life, there are all kinds of circumstances, but the law gives people no opportunities to make an excuse. So sometimes, people would break a law by doing something good.

6. **In many cultures there are stories about people who "rob from the rich to give to the poor". Do you think it's suitable to tell this kind of story to children?**

   — Well, it is OK to tell this as stories, but it is not really right to put them in textbooks. By listening to the stories, the children will learn to be nice to people, but they will have to learn everything else so that they can be able to tell right from wrong. In modern society, robbing from the rich to give to the poor is also illegal.

7. **Do you think it's morally right to have a death penalty?**

   —I think it depends, those who kill others purposely should be killed, but those innocent criminals should be given another opportunity. If there is no death penalty, many people would not be afraid of doing anything bad, because they know they would never die by doing bad things.

8. **Do you think most people in China abide by the law?**

   — Well, China is a big country with many people, so I have to say, it is impossible to make every one abide by the law, but most Chinese people are nice and can behave well. Anyway, no one would like to invite troubles.

9. **Can you suggest any way to solve the problem of people breaking the law?**

— Well, I think it is quite challenging to solve this problem, it is even unsolvable, but I think there are still something that we can do to make the situation better. For example, the government should establish a perfect law system, so that no one can take advantage of undeveloped law system. Secondly, all the children should get law education, so that they know what is right and what is illegal. Many people break the law because they did not know the law.

10. **What benefits are there for society when people obey the law?**

— If everyone obeys the law, society will be safer, and everyone will enjoy their life in the society. The government will not have to spend much money on enforcing the law, so the economy can be better developed.

11. **Why do you think some people break the law?**

— Well, it also depends on the situation. For some people, they break the law because they do not know the law; maybe they are victims of a broken family or of a previous crime. For some other people, they break the law, because they did something bad purposely, they might know the law very well, but they are taking risks. They are seduced by money or desire of something else.

12. **How do you think the police and lawyers play different roles in connection to law?**

— As I see it, they both play very important roles in enforcing the laws and making society safer, but they take different tasks in the same project. The police aim to find out the lawbreaker and the lawyer helps to prove the criminal guilty or innocent.

13. **What are the benefits of having international laws?**

— As the development of globalization, the international laws are becoming increasingly important, because people can travel around the world easily now and they can do business or committing crimes both at home and abroad, but the law system in each country of the world is different, so international laws are necessary to deal with crimes that are international.

14. **If there were no international laws, what do you think the world would be like?**

— Just like every country needs their law system, the world needs its laws as well. If there is no international laws, there will be more opportunities for the international crimes to develop, for example, drugs, deforestation and pollution etc. So people may be extinct soon.

15. **Do you think it is suitable to have the same laws for every country?**

— Not really, because every country has its own facts and culture, very often, the laws in one country might be something ridiculous in another country. However, the law that guarantees the basic human rights needs to be the same.

星期四

IT'S ALL ABOUT BUILDINGS

今天主要学习跟建筑相关的问题。其中第 1 部分的话题包括：house，room，building；第 2 部分学习描写 an important building；第 3 部分讨论与建筑相关的抽象问题。通过学习这些问题的范文和讲解，帮助考生回答关于建筑物话题的所有问题。

一、首先请根据下面的题目自测

Part 1	**Topic 1 House** 1. Do you live on your own, or do you live with your family? 2. What kind of house do you want to live in? 3. Do you like living with many people? **Topic 2 Room** 1. What do you put on the wall in your room? 2. How do you decorate your room? 3. What can you see from your window? **Topic 3 Building** 1. Do you like seeing the buildings when you are traveling? 2. What kind of architecture do you like? 3. Do you like the buildings in your school? 4. What is the most important building for you?
Part 2	Describe an important building in your hometown. You should say: where this building is what it looks like what it is used for and explain why it is important. **wrap-up questions:** 1. Do many tourists visit this building? 2. Do you think you will visit this building sometime soon?

（续）

Part 3	**Questions related to buildings** 1. Is it important to preserve old buildings? 2. do you think it's worth the money to preserve old buildings? 3. How have buildings changed in the past few years? 4. Compare old houses and modern houses. Which do people prefer to live in? 5. If everyone in China wanted to live in a big house with a garden, there would not be enough space for everyone. What is the solution to this problem? 6. Compare housing in Chinese cities and housing in villages. 7. What factors do people consider when deciding where to live? 8. How do you think the climate of a place affects the way buildings are constructed?

二、模板答案

Part 1

Topic 1 House

1. **Do you live on your own, or do you live with your family?**

— Well, I live in a three bedroom apartment with my parents. I have my own room, but I really want to move out.

2. **What kind of house do you want to live in?**

— Well, you know I quite like the nature, so I really hope that one day I can have my own house in the country side. I mean a house with a big garden, a swimming pool and many trees around the house.

3. **Do you like living with many people?**

— No, I much prefer to be quieter, because I need my privacy and more time of my own, I think living with many people would be quite annoying, and it will be very easy to have conflicts among family members.

Topic 2 Room

1. **What do you put on the wall in your room?**

— I do not like decorating rooms, so I've only put a picture of my idol on the front wall of my bedroom, so whenever I enter my room, I can see him, and I'm very happy. I think putting too many things on the wall may make the room felt crowded.

2. **How do you decorate your room?**

— As I have said, I have't put many thing on the wall, but I often have some fresh flowers in my room, so that I can feel warm and energetic.

3. **What can you see from your window?**

— You know I live on the 23rd floor of a building, so I can see many things from my window. I can have a bird's eye view of one third of this city, I can also see many birds flying in the sky.

Topic 3 Building

1. **Do you like seeing the buildings when you are traveling?**
   — Yes, I love architecture, I think it is fantastic to see the buildings of different styles, and there are always a lot of culture behind the different styles.
2. **What kind of architecture do you like?**
   — Well, I do not mind architecture style much, but I do enjoy seeing and living in the buildings that are of special features. Anyway, I just don't want to get lost in the places that are surrounded by the buildings that all look the same.
3. **Do you like the buildings in your school?**
   — Not really, I think they are too old, but not of the traditional style. They are just overused and are not very convenient to use. When I was studying there, I always hoped they could get the walls repainted at least.
4. **What is the most important building for you?**
   — The most important building is a small tower in a park of my hometown, because I spent a lot of time there when I was a kid. I would say, I had the most beautiful memory there, and every time, I think of that tower, I just feel warm, and feel at home.

Part 2

Describe an important building in your hometown.
You should say:
where this building is
what it looks like
what it is used for
and explain why it is important.

wrap-up questions:

1. Do many tourists visit this building?
2. Do you think you will visit this building sometime soon?

I would like to describe a group of buildings instead of one single building to you. It is the Forbiden City in Beijing.

Located on Chang'an Street, the Forbidden City is the symbolic building of Chinese ancient structure. It was built in the Ming dynasty, and has been rebuilt in the Qing dynasty as the home and office for the emperor. This palace shows its beauty by the historical red walls, the golden green roofs shine beautifully in the sunshine, the steps made of white marble, and the stone lions which seem to roar.

However, the real importance of the buildings is that it represents the history of the country and the city. Only if we bear the history in mind can we move on and have further development in all aspects.

Every year a lot of tourists from home and abroad come to visit this palace, so it is playing a very important role in the city's economy development, and with time going on, its importance is becoming more and more obvious.

Part 3 Questions related to buildings

1. **Is it important to preserve old buildings?**

   — I would say yes, because the old buildings are culture relics, which represent the historic development of architecture, economy, culture, etc. of a country. There are many benefits of preserving the old buildings, first of all, as I have mentioned above, that the old buildings can help to develop a city's economy, especially tourism. Secondly, it can give the descendents a better view of history.

2. **Do you think it's worth the money to preserve old buildings?**

   — Well, that is hard to tell. In my point of view, whether it is not worthy or not, I mean, we should not judge this by economic standard. There are many things that need to be done, but this does not mean, it may help to earn more money. It is just something that cannot be judged by money. More importantly, very often, the old buildings may help to earn money by attracting tourists.

3. **How have buildings changed in the past few years?**

   — I think architecture styles evolve very slowly; the buildings cannot be changed much in several years. But, there are still many changes that have taken place, especially on the inner decoration of the buildings. The buildings are modernized, I mean, they are all equipped with convenient tools, such as lift, and air-conditioning, and the constructing materials are greener now.

4. **Compare old houses and modern houses. Which do people prefer to live in?**

   — Well, I think both old houses and modern houses have their own advantages and disadvantages. But I much prefer to live in modern houses, because first of all, they are much safer to live in, because they are much better constructed with modern techniques and materials, and they are often more convenient because of its high tech-equipments.

5. **If everyone in China wanted to live in a big house with a garden, there would not be enough space for everyone. What is the solution to this problem?**

   — I think that is too big a question for me to answer, but I think something can be done. First of all, the government should help to develop the outskirts or even rural areas, so that people would not only just come into the cities, they can actually have a very good life in non-urban areas. More importantly, the number of people needs to be controlled, many problems result from over population, if there are always too many people, the problems can never be solved.

6. **Compare housing in Chinese cities and housing in villages.**

— There are too many differences between the Chinese cities and villages. Here I would only mention several of them. For example, the education in the cities is much more developed than that in the countryside, and the traffic is much more convenient. However, the villager can enjoy more fresh air, more free time and would seldom worry about being in a traffic jam on the way.

7. **What factors do people consider when deciding where to live?**

— There are many factors to consider when choosing a place to settle down. First of all, the work place of the family members is the most essential factor. People would normally choose to work close to where they live, because in China, normally, a job might be very long or even lifelong. Another factor that people often consider is the consumption cost and the facilities that a place has. Everybody wants to live a more comfortable life.

8. **How do you think the climate of a place affects the way buildings are constructed?**

— The climate may have a great influence on how people construct their buildings. For example, in the north, it is generally very cold, so people would have to install heating systems, and they have to make the rooms shorter and the walls thicker, so that it is easier to keep the room warm. However, in the south, it could be terribly hot or stuffy, so they would generally consider having more windows and bigger doors, so that they can keep them open in summer. Also because of the climate, the materials people use to build houses are different, in the south, more wood and bamboo would be used, while in the north, people would choose to use more stones and bricks.

星期五

IT'S ALL ABOUT COURSES

今天主要学习跟课程相关的问题。其中第 1 部分的话题包括：teacher，course，children education；第 2 部分学习描写 a short-term course；第 3 部分讨论与课程相关的抽象问题。通过学习这些问题的范文和讲解，帮助考生回答关于课程学习话题的所有问题。

一、首先请根据下面的题目自测

Part 1	**Topic 1 Teachers** 1. Have you ever thought of being a teacher? 2. Do students in China respect teachers? 3. What qualities should a good teacher have? 4. Which teacher has influenced you the most? **Topic 2 Course** 1. Do you like studying? 2. Which subjects do you like best in your school time? 3. What courses do you think are the most useful one for you? 4. Do you think the courses you take in university are useful? **Topic 3 Children's education** 1. Do you think every child should learn arts/swimming/ singing? 2. What kind of subjects do you think children should take?
Part 2	Describe a short-term course or class that you took. You should say: what this class or course was how long you attended this course or class where you took this course or class and explain how you felt about the course or class. **wrap-up questions:** ● Do you recommend this course?
Part 3	**Questions related to education** 1. What do you think is the value of education? 2. Compare the value of knowledge gained from books to knowledge gained from practical experience in the workplace. 3. Do you think it's a good idea to have classes without examinations? 4. How do you think education will change in the future? 5. What is the value of adult education? 6. Why do graduates in some specializations find work more easily than graduates with other specializations? 7. Do you plan to further your education after you graduate?

二、模板答案

Part 1

Topic 1 Teachers

1. **Have you ever thought of being a teacher?**

— No, not really, I don't think I can be a teacher. I am not really patient, and I am not good at explaining things to people.

2. **Do students in China respect teachers?**

— Yes, I think so, although they cannot be compared with people in ancient times. People still respect teachers. We compare teachers with spiritual gardener, who cultivate talents for the country.

3. **What qualities should a good teacher have?**

— Well, it is not easy to be a teacher, because there are many requirements for a qualified teacher. First of all, a teacher should be knowledgeable, more importantly, a teacher needs to have good morals, and sometimes needs to be humorous.

4. **Which teacher has influenced you the most?**

— Frankly speaking, I am very lucky. I have come across many good teachers and many of them had great influence on me, but the one that influences me the most is the class master in my senior high school. He not only taught me knowledge, but also made me a good person, I am very grateful to him.

Topic 2 Course

1. **Do you like studying?**

— Not really, I do not like sitting for long, so my teachers often thought that I was a bad student, but I do like reading, especially novels and magazines.

2. **Which subjects do you like best in your school time?**

— When I was a school boy, I quite liked sciences, so my favorite subjects at that time were physics and chemistry; I thought they were magical and mysterious.

3. **What courses do you think are the most useful one for you?**

— I think most of the courses I have taken are quite useful, but the most useful one was English, because it has had a very big influence on me, and it is going to influence me in the future.

4. **Do you think the courses you take in university are useful?**

— Not really, in university I have taken many courses. Some are theoretical, some are practical and there are also some political courses, I don't think they are useful, because I would never use them.

Topic 3 Children's education

1. **Do you think every child should learn arts/swimming/ singing?**
   — It is true that if a child know something about arts/swimming/singing, they would be advantageous in their future life and work, but I don't think every child should learn that, because people are different. As for what to learn, it should be determined by people's interest and aptitude.

2. **What kind of subjects do you think children should take?**
   — To be frank, I am not sure what subjects children should take, but I do think it is very necessary for them to learn something that enables them to be creative.

Part 2

Describe a short-term course or class that you took. You should say: what this class or course was how long you attended this course or class where you took this course or class and explain how you felt about the course or class.

wrap-up questions:

- Do you recommend this course?

I would like to describe a short-term course I have taken last year. It is a computer course. To be more specific, I learned how to make PowerPoint files.

Since I graduated last year, and I was lucky to get a job right after my graduation, but the job requirements said that I would have to do presentations to customers, which means I would have to make PowerPoint files. I had never learnt that before, so I had to take a course.

I took registered immediately, and had a one-hour class every evening, and it lasted for about one month. I have learnt a lot in that course. For example, I have learnt the principles of how to make a PowerPoint file outstanding, and how to attract the attention of my audience, as well as how to combine it with multi-media resources. I enjoyed that course a lot.

And I have benefited a lot too, because right after I started my job, I had to make many presentations with PowerPoint, so what I have learnt in that course helped me a lot.

Part 3 Questions related to education

1. **What do you think is the value of education?**
   — Wow, I think that is a very big question. Education is very valuable, first of all, it

enlightens people and helps people to transfer knowledge from generation to generation. It also makes people kind and civilized. To sum up, if there is no education, human beings will still be in the aboriginal state.

2. **Compare the value of knowledge gained from books to knowledge gained from practical experience in the workplace.**

— For any learner, knowledge from both books and practical experience is necessary, the book knowledge enables us to know more about the world, and hands-on experience makes us able to handle things in the right way.

3. **Do you think it's a good idea to have classes without examinations?**

— No, I don't think so. As a student, I hate examinations, but I hate them because most of them are boring and terrible, not because of its existence. I mean, examinations are necessary, but we need to make it valid and reliable.

4. **How do you think education will change in the future?**

— Great changes have taken place on education, I think education will continue to change. In future, the concepts of teachers will be changed, teachers will not only be instructors, they would have to be more competence, so that they can use the modern technology to teach. What's more, the purpose of education will be changed as well, I think the purpose of education will not only be career-oriented, there must be some other purposes.

5. **What is the value of adult education?**

— With the development of science and technology, I think life-long learning is very important, so adult education will be very valuable. Adults need to keep learning no matter what kind of jobs they take. It is going to be a very important compliment for higher education.

6. **Why do graduates in some specializations find work more easily than graduates with other specializations?**

— Well, I think there are many reasons contributing to that phenomenon. First of all, the market is a very iomportant factor, some specializations are in greater demand, of course, and they would find it easier. Also, the quality of university education is a key element, some specializations are very developed or mature, so they can get the graduates ready for their future career, but some other university cannot do equally well.

7. **Do you plan to further your education after you graduate?**

— Yes, I suppose so, but firstly, I would like to get a job, so that I would know what is my real interest and need, so that I can choose the right orientation and have a purpose. I will study better.

星期六

IT'S ALL ABOUT CHANGES

人的一生要经历无数变化。关于人生的各种变化，在雅思口语考试中频频出现。但很多考生因为没有思考过这些问题，对此觉得十分棘手。今天主要学习跟人生变化相关的问题。其中第1部分的话题包括：change，your change，social change；第2部分学习描写a recent change；第3部分讨论与人生变化相关的抽象问题。通过学习这些问题的范文和讲解，帮助考生回答关于变化话题的所有问题。

一、首先请根据下面的题目自测

Part 1	**Topic 1 Change** 1. Do you like changes? 2. What are the changes that everyone needs to face? 3. What are the changes that are hard to take? 4. What kind of people do not like changes much? **Topic 2 Your change** 1. What changes have taken place in your spare time activities? 2. What changes have taken place in your personality? 3. What are the differences between the color you like now and that in your childhood? **Topic 3 Social change** 1. What changes have taken place in your living environment? 2. What changes have taken place in the last decade in your hometown? 3. Do you like these changes? 4. What are the changes that you do not like?
Part 2	Describe a recent change that changed your life in a good way. You should say: what the change was what caused this change what the result of this change was and explain how you felt about this change when it happened. **wrap-up questions:** 1. Did your family support your decision? 2. Were your parents pleased with this change?
Part 3	**Questions related to changes** 1. Do you think change is good in people's lives? 2. Why are old people generally unwilling to make changes in their life? 3. How could a parent help a child be prepared to cope with future change? 4. What are some of the factors leading to change in people's lives?

（续）

Part 3	5. What are some advantages and some disadvantages of living your whole life in one place? 6. What do you think of working for one company all your life? 7. In your opinion, is it a good thing to change jobs often? 8. Do you think change and development are always the same thing? 8. Has the computer changed your life very much?

二、模板答案

Part 1

Topic 1 Change

1. Do you like changes?

— Well, it depends on what kind of change. I quite like the changes in my job. I hate doing the same thing every day. But I do not like the changes in my life, such as living environment, friends, and family and so on. I hope to have them all the time.

2. What are the changes that everyone needs to face?

— Life is full of changes. For every individual, he/she has to face the changes like growing up, meeting different people and separating with people. Get jobs, change jobs, and become a family member of another family, become parents, and so on. We can never stop the process of change.

3. What are the changes that are hard to take?

—There are many changes that are hard to take, for example, when we grow up, we have to separate with friends, we have to face death of the dearest people. Oh, there is one more, I mean, we will become old one day.

4. What kind of people do not like changes much?

— Well, I think that is hard to say, but generally the elder people do not like changes, they prefer much more stable life.

Topic 2 Your change

1. What changes have taken place in your spare time activities?

— Well, I don't know. I have never thought about it, let me see. I think I go out more often when I was younger, and I had more gatherings with friends years ago. What's more, I spend much less time on spare time activities now, because I have a very busy schedule.

2. What changes have taken place in your personality?

— I think I haven't changed much, but when I was a school boy, I was very shy, I did not talk much, I especially felt shy talking with girls, but right now, I am very outgoing, and I have many friends.

3. What are the differences between the color you like now and that in your childhood?

— When I was in my childhood, I liked light colors such as yellow and green, but right now, I much prefer dark colors, which I think are more mature. Although my favorite color is always blue.

Topic 3 Social change

1. What changes have taken place in your living environment?

— Well, you know I live in Beijing, and the living environment has been changed greatly in the last several years. First of all, the air is much fresher, and there are more green areas now, more importantly, the traffic condition has been changed a lot, and I can go anywhere I want very easily.

2. What changes have taken place in the last decade in your hometown?

— In my hometown, great changes have taken place in the last decade. For example, people's living standards have been greatly improved, and people are more open minded now, it is becoming very convenient for living. To be more specific, the traffic conditions have been improved, and more people could afford private cars, and there are more and more skyscrapers. I think I can never finish telling the changes.

3. Do you like these changes?

— Yes, definitely, because all these changes enable people to have more comfortable life, and with all these changes, people can actually try to be in line with people in the big cities and the people in other counties.

4. What are the changes that you do not like?

— With all the good changes, there are some minor changes that are not pleasant. For example, it seems that people are not as close as years ago. While people are improving their living standards, the amount of happiness they get is not increasing, and sometimes, it is reducing, which is a shame.

Part 2

Describe a recent change that changed your life in a good way.

You should say:

what the change was

what caused this change

what the result of this change was

and explain how you felt about this change when it happened.

wrap-up questions:

1. Did your family support your decision?
2. Were your parents pleased with this change?

Recently, there is a great change that has taken place in my life. I had a baby girl, and I became a father. I think it might be the very best change for me after my marriage.

This change has almost changed my entire life, for good or bad, I like them all.

Since the baby was born, I was busier, but happier. All of a sudden, all the tiredness has gone away, and all the responsibilities that I need to taken are welcomed. Thinking that I should be hard working and try my best to give her whatever I can, I have never been so motivated to work.

More importantly, being a father makes me more mature, because now I have to consider more for whatever I am doing, and whatever I do, I would have to remind myself that I am a father now, I will reevaluate the things I do.

Looking at the angel like face, I feel that I am the luckiest man in the world. I do not complain as much as before. I treasure all the things I have. I try to take all the things in a positive way.

Anyway, becoming a father is the best change I have ever had.

Part 3 Questions related to changes

1. **Do you think change is good in people's lives?**

— Sure, although there are good and bad changes, but only with changes, can people move on and try to have better lives. Life can be taken as a process of perusing better life or better changes. But if there is no change, people might not have the motivation to do all the things they are doing with changes.

2. **Why are old people generally unwilling to make changes in their life?**

— Generally speaking, elder people much prefer a stable life, because very often changes means they would have to change their own way of doing things, which may cause a lot of inconvenience to them. For example, they would have to separate with their friends, or family, or even all the things they are accustomed to. So they may not have sense of security.

3. **How could a parent help a child be prepared to cope with future change?**

— Well, helping a child be prepared to cope with future changes means to enable them to handle things by themselves. So it is important not to be overprotective, the children need to do things with their own hands and get enough practice. Or to put it into another way, do not only give children things. Instead, parents need to give children ways of doing things.

4. **What are some of the factors leading to change in people's lives?**

— There are many factors that might lead to change in people's lives. For example, the policy and laws of the government, the economy development, the interpersonal relationship, the family finance condition and employment etc. It seems that all the changes taken place in the world might have some influence and lead to change in people's lives.

5. **What are some advantages and some disadvantages of living your whole life in one place?**

— Living in one place for an entire life might have many advantages, for example, people can keep all the friends and relatives in contact, and all these interpersonal connections may mean a more secure life, because people may always help each other. But living in one place, at the same time, means there is little change for one's life, and they might miss a lot of opportunities for having a better life.

6. **What do you think of working for one company all your life?**

— Well, there are many disadvantages of working for one company for my entire life, but I would much prefer that to keep changing jobs. Because if I work only in one company, I will be more motivated, because I know it is my only job and I have no other opportunities. And if I only work in one company, all the things I am doing today might be of use tomorrow. Finally, working for only one company saves me a lot of energy, because I do not have to think about changing jobs, which means, I can spend more time working.

7. **In your opinion, is it a good thing to change jobs often?**

— Well, I think it might be good to change jobs for two or three times, but to change jobs too often might have negative influence in one's life. First of all, if one keeps changing jobs, it will be very difficult for him or her to have a very high position, because every time before he or she gets promoted, they might have changed their jobs already. And keep changing might have negative influence on their job hunting, because the next employer may think that he or she can never work for a long time in one company.

8. **Do you think change and development are always the same thing?**

— Not really, changes might be good and bad, but development is very often good change. For example, if someone lost his job, or get laid off, it is a change for him, but it is not development, although he might have another opportunity to develop himself.

9. **Has the computer changed your life very much?**

— It is not exaggerating to say that computers have changed my life entirely. They have changed my way of working, now I seldom use paper and pen, and I rely on the Internet a lot. Computers have changed my life style a lot, I seldom go shopping now, because I only shop online, I also take a course online instead of going to schools. And I keep contact with friends mainly through the Internet. In short, I cannot live without computers any more.

星期日

IT'S ALL ABOUT JOBS

不管你是否已经工作，工作这个话题总是雅思口语考官很青睐的一个话题。如果你还没有工作，他们就会问你的理想和对未来工作的打算是什么；如果你正在工作，他们就会跟你谈论你现有的工作和换工作等。这个话题出现频率非常高，所以应该引起重视。对于没有工作的考生来说，更是要好好准备。在今天的学习内容中，第 1 部分的话题包括：job，unemployment，position；第 2 部分学习描写 a job you are good at；第 3 部分讨论与工作相关的抽象问题。通过学习这些问题的范文和讲解，以提高顺利回答关于工作话题的所有问题的能力。

一、首先请根据下面的题目自测

Part 1	**Topic 1 Job** 1. How long have you been working? 2. What do you usually do in your office? 3. What are the main skills needed for your work? 4. What is the best thing about your job? **Topic 2 Unemployment** 1. Is there much unemployment in your country? 2. What do you think are the causes of this? 3. What do you suggest could be done to ease this problem? **Topic 3 Position** 1. What is your position now in your company? 2. Do you prefer to be a leader or an ordinary staff? 3. What qualities do you think a manager needs to have? 4. Do you think every staff should try to be managers?
Part 2	Describe a job you think you would be good at. You should say: what job it would be what skills you would need to do this job how you would get this job and explain why you think you would be able to do this job well. **wrap-up questions:** ● Do you know anyone who is doing this job?
Part 3	**Questions related to jobs** 1. (In China), what factors influence people's choice when they decide what work to do? 2. Do boys and girls generally choose the same types of careers? 3. What advice (or suggestions) would you give to young people who are trying to choose a career?

（续）

Part 3	4. Do you think it would be suitable for university students in China to study part-time and also do part-time work, at the same time? 5. What kinds of work are the most popular choices for young people today? 6. What careers would you say have high social status in your country? 7. Do you agree that everyone in society should receive the same salary? 8. Do you think changing your job is a positive thing to do? 9. Why do you think it's harder for an older person to change their job? 10. What do you think are the qualities of a "good employee"?

二、模板答案

Part 1

Topic 1 Job

1. **How long have you been working?**

— I have worked for about 5 years, although this is the first year in my present job.

2. **What do you usually do in your office?**

— Well, I do not have a very stable routine, because my work is very flexible, but generally speaking, I would have to check my emails and have appointments with my clients, and have meetings. Oh, yes, a lot of phone calls.

3. **What are the main skills needed for your work?**

— Well, you know I am a sales manager, I need a lot of skills to do my work well. Firstly I need to be good with the computer and Internet, because almost all the work is done on computer and through the Internet. Also, I need to be able to use foreign languages, because half of my clients are from other countries, and I need to communicate with them, and not all of them can speak English. Finally, I need to be good at sports, especially golf, because I have to entertain my clients.

4. **What is the best thing about your job?**

— As for me, the best thing about my job is that I can be flexible in the time, I mean, I do not have to work from nine to five, what I need to do is to get things done, and I don't have to be in the office all the time. And no line manager would bother to interfere with what I do, what they want is just results, if I can get products sold, they would be very happy.

Topic 2 Unemployment

1. **Is there much unemployment in your country?**

— Yes, I think so, especially in big cities, there are many university graduates unemployed.

2. **What do you think are the causes of this?**

— I think this is a very complex issue, caused by many factors. For example, the market do not need so many people anymore, because there is much work that was traditionally done by humans is now done by machines. Also, the international competition makes the situation worse.

3. **What do you suggest could be done to ease this problem?**

— Well, this is a problem that almost every country is facing, and it seems there is no perfect solution, but I think there is still something that can be done to ease the problem. First of all, the government should try to create employment opportunities for people, and all the people need to open their mind, I mean they do not have to be employed, they can employ themselves, but the government should give them help for them to set up their own business, so that they can help themselves and many others be employed.

Topic 3 Position

1. **What is your position now in your company?**

— I am now working as a manager in the human resource department in my company. I am mainly in charge of staff training.

2. **Do you prefer to be a leader or an ordinary staff?**

— I think both have their benefits and drawbacks, but I think to be a leader is more advantageous, because it means that I might have more power and can have more opportunities to realize my own ideas, and if I work hard, I can help more people and the company to realize their dreams.

3. **What qualities do you think a manager needs to have?**

— I think a manager needs to have many qualities, first of all, he or she needs to be open-minded, I mean, they need to keep learning, so that they can always make sure their managing is effective. Secondly, a good manager needs to be cooperative, because he or she would have to cooperate with all the other managers, their staff and clients. Finally, a manager needs to have leadership, because he or she would direct the company to the right direction.

4. **Do you think every staff should try to be managers?**

— Well, there is a saying which says that the soldier who does not want to be a general is not a good soldier. I just cannot agree with that point of view. On the contrary, I think every staff needs to know that not everyone can be a manager and not everyone needs to be a manager, people in different positions are necessary and important, what they need to know is whatever position they take, they should try their best to do it well.

Part 2

Describe a job you think you would be good at.

You should say:

what job it would be

what skills you would need to do this job

how you would get this job

and explain why you think you would be able to do this job well.

wrap-up questions:

- Do you know anyone who is doing this job?

I think I will be a good doctor.

In my opinion, to be a good doctor I need to be patient, responsible and well educated.

First of all, I am a very easy going and kind person. I can be very patient. I seldom lose my temper. I think if I were a doctor, I would be very patient with all the patients.

Secondly, I am very responsible. I think to be a doctor, being responsible is the number one quality, because only if the doctor is responsible, will he be serious to his job and consider as much as he can for the patients.

Finally, a doctor needs to be well educated. If I want to be a doctor, I need to first of all get a doctor's degree, I mean eight years in university and another several years in clinic, so that I can be experienced enough to deal with all the health problems my patients have, and can figure out a solution for them.

Anyway, to be a doctor is not easy, but I think I am quite suitable to be a doctor if I make good use of my personality and study hard.

Part 3 Questions related to jobs

1. **(In China), what factors influence people's choice when they decide what work to do?**

   — I think people all around the world would generally choose their job by considering salary, professional development and their own interests. although there are many other elements that might influence one's decision of choosing a job.First of all, how much money one can make by taking the job is the most essential factor, because the salary is often the standard people use to judge if a job is decent or not.Secondly, professional development prediction plays a very important role, because no one would take a job and do the same thing for their whole life. Everyone would expect to have some development in their profession, so that they can be better and better.Finally, people would consider how happy they would be if they took that job, I mean, they need to know if they are interested in that job or not.

2. **Do boys and girls generally choose the same types of careers?**

   — Well, gender difference is becoming less and less obvious in modern society when choosing a job or career. On the contrary, gender balance is becoming increasingly important in almost every field, because people can do the job well, no matter which sex the staff is.

3. **What advice (or suggestions) would you give to young people who are trying to choose a career?**

   — Well, I am quite young myself, but I would strongly suggest those who are hunting for a job not to take money as the only criteria to choose a job, because for whatever job they take, they could not be well paid in the very beginning, and all the jobs would give them more and more economic payback, so they would have to analyze themselves and make sure what kind of job they suit, and how far they can go if they take a certain job.

4. **Do you think it would be suitable for university students in China to study part-time and also do part-time work, at the same time?**

— Well, I personally think it is a good idea, because in China, senior high school graduates go directly to universities, without any social practice, actually many university students do not know what they will do and what is really needed to do that job well, and many university graduates cannot work independently because they lack practices. Therefore, if the students take part-time job, they would gradually get some work experience and get ready for their future career, and by doing the jobs, they would know what they need to learn in the universities.

5. **What kinds of work are the most popular choices for young people today?**

— Well, the most popular choices for young people today are those risky, but rich ones. The young generation pay special attention to quick success, they are not as patient as the former generation, they cannot wait for decades for their success.

6. **What careers would you say have high social status in your country?**

— In China, the government officials or civil servants generally have very high social status, because they have power in their hands, and they can do many things that others can't. Apart from that, lawyers and doctors enjoy high social status, anyway, anybody that can do things that are crucial can be very respected.

7. **Do you agree that everyone in society should receive the same salary?**

— Not really. I think the amount of money people get should be determined by how much contribution they have done to the company or the society. Only if that can people be motivated to be hard working, and only if they are paid differently, can it be fair, and can the society be stable.

8. **Do you think changing your job is a positive thing to do?**

— Well, that depends. Right now, I am not thinking of changing my job, because I quite enjoy doing this job, and it is well paid, and I can get lots of things done everyday. I think it is rather good. If I have to change it, I would feel very bad, and it would definitely be a negative thing to do.

9. **Why do you think it's harder for an older person to change their job?**

— It is generally hard for elder people to change jobs, because most companies would have an age limit on the candidates. Older people are generally considered experienced, but not creative, nor open-minded, therefore it is harder for them to find a job. As for the older people themselves, they do not like changes much, so they much prefer to keep their own job.

10. **What do you think are the qualities of a "good employee"?**

— Almost all the employers would be critical when managing employees, so it is rather difficult to be a good employee. But, generally, good employees are motivated, and they are willing to do anything that may improve their work. Secondly, good employees need to keep learning, so that they can always be able to handle the things arising in the company. What's more, good employees should always take the company as their own business, so that they would consider all the details to make it good.